The
Pastor
Dilemma
Staying True to a Biblical Style of Preaching

Nollen Elzie Sr. PhD

ISBN: 978-1-7336754-6-8

Liberation's Publishing LLC
West Point, Mississippi
www.liberationspublishing.com

The
Pastor
Dilemma

Staying True to a Biblical Style of Preaching

Nollen Elzie Sr. PhD

Table of Content

Preface

I am very grateful for the patience of the Zion Spring Missionary Baptist Church family of Okolona, Mississippi where I am privileged to serve as pastor. I want to thank the survey responders Gregory Stephen, Nikita Quinn, Emma Bailey, Lamonica Calvert, for their attentiveness and honesty during the sermon survey. I gratefully want to thank Cremolia Ann Wren thoughtful prayers and encouragement. A special prayer and thanks will continuously be in my spirit for Dr. Jeffrey A. Gladney for his support. A Special thanks to my sister Margret Judy (Elzie) Duncan and her spiritual inspiration in my life.

Above all I'm extremely thankful for my wife, Bettie Joyce (Taylor) Elzie for giving up special times and events, thus allowing me the needed time for this doctrinal challenge at the Newburgh Theological Seminary and College of the Bible and the writing of this book. To my sons Nollen Kirk Elzie Jr, and Jason Cortez Elzie, I love you.

Introduction

There are certain challenges that Christian leaders, especially those called to the office of pastor, are perpetually faced with. It is the challenge of keeping the gospel relevant in a world every changing and becoming more and more dependent on itself only. There is a false sense of safety in this "information" age of microwave answers and gratification, because the moral calamity still exists that was first imparted into man in the Garden of Eden.

Man being the crowning glory of God's creation became corrupted, plummeting the entire world into the darkness of sin. Adam's lack of adherence to the command of God is recorded in the book of Genesis chapter three. So catastrophic was this act of disobedience that God in his omniscient remedied the situation before the founding of the world, while in time, He remedied the situation by divinely sending and offering up His only Begotten Son (the homogeneous) His "unique holy other" Jesus Christ, as a blood sacrifice for the salvation of the fallen race.

As a perpetual reminder and extender of this gift of salvation, God instituted humans to further fulfill His divine prerogative of calling men to become his voice and the medium in the world for preaching to the world of old and to come, the birth, death, burial, resurrection and ascension of His Son Jesus the Christ. Thus, offering salvation and a renewed relationship between God and man.

How does one keep the need for a Savior in the forefront of a world that appears to save itself? This dilemma weighs heavily on pastors for it is a challenge to keep Christ relevant while staying true to biblical teachings. Each chapter will unfold God's great drama of salvation through the voices and lives of men labeled as pastoral leaders. This will allow one to take a panoramic view of the workings of ancient leaders from days of old up until know, which in turn will manifest a biblical style of preaching that can be reproduced in the twenty-first century.

Chapter One: The Proper Perspective

Preaching God's Word in a contemporary environment in a time when crisis abound in churches is challenging. That coupled with the work of pastoral care in areas where ineffective Christian ministries plague the twenty first century church communities the challenge is doubled. Having said that, Gary McIntosh and Glen Martin argue, "...Many churches have created more of a country club than an army...."[1] Dr. Brent Largent conducted a seminar offered as a curriculum through Newburgh Theological Seminary Master's Program, he observed "God works in us to carry out His Word."[2] Presenting preaching as God's spiritual instrument used by those who called was God's way to proclaim the gospel of Jesus Christ and accomplish the primary goals of biblical preaching which is to reach lost souls for the Kingdom of God. Even though the styles of preaching vary in different demographical regions among church communities in general they still had the same result. Attributing to

---

[1] McIntosh, Gary, Glenn Martin, *Finding Them, Keeping: Effective Strategies for Evangelism and Assimilation in the Local Church.* Nashville, TN: Broadman & Holman Publishers 1992 p. 44
[2] Largent, Brent (Seminar) *Survey of First and Second Thessalonians,* Theological Studies, Newburgh Theological Seminary and College of the Bible: Evansville, Indiana 2009. Web. 11 April, 2011. www.newburghseminary.com

these variations of preaching styles are general education, and seminary training among ministers, as well as church community's readiness to receive persons whom God sends as pastoral leaders. Many challenging issues for a new generation of preachers seem more pronounced than those of their previous predecessors some 40 years ago. The cumulative information collected addresses ministerial views of the biblical style approach of preaching. It devolves pastoral style leadership of preaching from a biblical-Christian context.

In today's commercial driven culture, the industrial community has become proficient at producing products at lightning speed. The use of molds or patterns of all styles and shapes to produce a wide range of manufactured goods used has made production effortless. These molds are useful for shaping object to be used for industrialization of modern-day society. Christianity coexists in an information age of computerized wonderism, where information is readily available in nanoseconds. It is designed to educate and inform the electronically connected community in all segments of the developed world on a daily basis.

However, God uses the method of divinely revealing Himself through His Word. In etymology the word *Logos* appears in Greek terminology refers to root "word." To reveal the divineness of God He calls special messengers for that purpose. For instance, these messengers were called prophets. They first appeared in the Old Testament. This title is from the Hebrew word" *nabi*" and in the New Testament a verbal expression is used called *"Kerusso"* which is to proclaim the Word with the voice. Revealing means to present the revelation of God in the preached word.

The church is constantly transitioning and transforming as God's instrument on earth to address the changing times of twenty first century culture. It is imperative that pastors involved in pastoral ministry and biblical preaching for today's leadership rethink and realign their approach to reaching the present generation. However, redefining biblical preaching is not necessary. What it does mean is the role of pastoral leadership must remain faithful to God's prophetic calling of preaching a biblical based gospel through expounding on the logos.

Developing a specific style of preaching requires adhering to the Scriptural call of preaching. Preachers must keep in mind that their calling is from God. Their goal is to become biblical leaders while developing into spiritual pastoral leader. In doing so, they must not view themselves as mass-produced mouth pieces freshly from the halls of theological seminaries, but as spiritual prophetic agents of God, going through the process of growing into faithful ministers of the Lord Jesus Christ.

Preachers are molded and shaped by the Holy Spirit who in turn develop them into quality Christian servants whom God ordains and sanctions as His proclaimers of His Gospel. Preachers do themselves a grave disservice by not attaching themselves in their formative years to a godly minister or seasoned pastor whose leadership style is that of demonstrating biblical preaching. A godly leader is one who follows the good example of the gospel of Jesus

13

Christ. The ideal of preaching hinges on proper tutoring which aids in the shaping for pastoral service, and also forms effective ministers of the pulpit duty.

God does allow many hurts and heartbreaks to occur in ministers' lives in order to develop them spiritually. The truth of the matter is these afflictions are a means of transforming them into the image, the spiritual likeness of Jesus Christ. Therefore, as proclaimers of the Gospel they develop an internal philosophy of the basics of preaching. God implementing spiritual strength through the tests of life. One will also discover in the field of pastoral ministry that many of those challenging ordeals are designed to encourage a certain spiritual paradigm shift to help ministers of the gospel abandon much of the world's culture. They replace worldly views to cultivate Christian faith views as a means of transforming and transitioning into spiritual servants God intended for His preachers of the gospel to become.

The Scripture affirms, "I beseech you therefore, brethren, by the mercies of God, that ye present your bodies a living sacrifice, holy, acceptable unto God, which is your reasonable service. And be not conformed to this world: but be ye transformed by the renewing of your mind, that ye may prove what is that good, and acceptable, and perfect, will of God" (Romans 12:1-2, KJV[3]).

Samuel L. Bowman in a sermon work, *Preaching in the Capital* said, "The work of the gospel is most solemn and

---

[3] Romans 12: 1-2 King James Bible

important…How desirable to be rightly furnished the Holy calling; and so to labor in it, that we may make full proof of our ministry, that at last we may receive from the hand of the Great Shepherd the crown of glory that fadeth not away."[4] In fact, the Holy Spirit partners with called men of God as the internal guide and source of pastoral ministers. Holy Spirit comes from the Greek word *parakaloe,* meaning "to call to one's side." The gospel acknowledges the presences of the Holy Spirit, the third person of the trinity in the Godhead as the messenger, enabler which says, "But the Counselor, the Holy Spirit, whom the Father will send in my name, will teach you all things and will remind you of everything I have said to you" (John 14:26-27, NIV)[5].

Therefore, it is of necessity that getting a handle on the reason for a biblical style of pastoral preaching, its artful presentation, and its purpose. The pastor/preacher have an obligation to develop a style of preaching that involves reflecting, powerful thinking, and adopting a powerful understanding of the Word of God to fulfill the calling upon their lives as ministers and servants of God. Jerry Vine and Jim Shaddix when referring to the Gospel argue, "God's messengers were men who brought good

---

[4] Bowman, Samuel L. *Preaching in the Capital.* Nashville, Tennessee: Sunday School Publishing Board National Baptist Convention, U. S. A., Inc., 1993. p 149

[5] John 14: 26-27 New International Version

news. A parallel word in the New Testament is *evangelize*, "to announce glad tiding"[6]

In other words, the art of presenting the good news of the gospel must be developed in the ministers of God. They must have the attributes of powerful thinking and the mentality of powerful understanding. Not being readily equipped or not possessing these mental abilities does not make the messengers of the preaching community any less ministers of the gospel of Jesus Christ; it only means they will need to vigorously rely on the aid of Holy Spirit and become disciplined in the ministerial habits.

Those who do arrive to the point in ministry of enjoying the awesome task of imparting the spiritual truths of God to the Christian Community develop a deep concern for lost sinners.

Whereas, preaching and pastoring the Word of God in a new millennium, every minister experience the tug of reshaping by the Holy Spirit to become more like Christ and a better leader. The Holy Spirit, the third person of the Triune, is at work as the every present Helper. He is indwelling, walking along side and influencing the servants of God. It is through Him that God molds us to move us. It is through His molding that God makes all preachers and pastors His usable servants.

Preaching in today's church while presenting Jesus Christ in a society of an ever-changing toxic culture places tremendous stress

---

[6] Vines, Jerry, and Jim Shaddix. *Power in the Pulpit: How to Prepare and Deliver Expository Sermons.* Chicago: MOODY PUBLISHERS, 1999. p. 21

upon preachers of the Gospel. Shadowing pastors devoted to the work of pastoral care, not only must they labor as leaders in the toxic environment they must also present a biblical style of preaching conducive to the care of the local church communities.

Traditional pastors maintaining Christian views of preaching are faced with the dilemma of preaching Jesus' birth, death, burial, resurrection and ascension against many many false religions. They imitate Christianity and disguise new tactics in its attempt to discredit the gospel. In other words, false religions camouflage its work with modern spins in their presentations and go under the guise of true Christian religion and in an effort to derail the divine mandated purpose of God and His Church.

World views challenge biblical truths with great tenacity. Therefore, it is for these reasons that pastoral ministry and preachers of the gospel community must mandate for themselves a biblical style of preaching for Jesus Christ. The twenty-first century pastoral ministry needs and deserves clarity in the preaching experience during these last days of the eminent return of Jesus Christ of reclaiming His church.

A biblical style of preaching the gospel in a twenty-first culture demands it because of an intensified attack on the validity of the Bible, Christianity, and its Author, God. In fact, as early as 2007 the socialist, and atheist Christopher Hitchens authored a book, *God is not Great: How Religion Poisons Everything with a New Afterword.* In it he asserts, "…My parents did not try to impose any religion: I was probably fortunate in having a father who not especially loved his strict Baptist/Calvinist up-bringing, and a mother who preferred assimilating partly for my sake...I know enough about all religions to know that I would always be an infidel at all times and in all places."[7]

In light of the atheistic worldview, pastoral preachers in the community cannot take the work of the gospel message ministry lightly. A pastoral self-prerequisite of the ministerial call to the Gospel is a personal issue and priority of every Christian preacher of the Gospel and of every ecclesiastical church leader.

Advisedly, even the most devote believer should make public statements affirming the call to preach the gospel that they have received confirmation from the God. Preaching for God is unexplainable. Believers receive such an unction from the Holy Spirit. They will know the overpowering revelation of God's purpose within. It is something that one simply knows.

Preaching, for the novice is a kind of unsettling spiritual gnawing, tugging and tearing at the soul. Ultimately, the best external discerners of the Christian faith are a church's congregations. Many times, they are the ones who may have picked up on or seen some spiritual signs of a preaching candidate's call. In the end, it will be the minister who must know for certainty, without doubt that God has initiated the preaching or pastoral of this spiritual

---

[7] Hitchens, Christopher *god is not Great: How Religion Poisons Everything*, Twelve New York, NY, 2007, p. 11

vocation. The business of pastoral ministry is an area of understanding only another preacher can explain or understand.

Ministry like it or not will always be challenged by worldviews. On the other hand, defenders of the gospel deliberately and with purpose proclaim Jesus the Christ as the Savior of lost sinners. He is the Suffering Servant of the redeemed and present Jesus as the Son of the living God who is the hope and spiritual Father of all saints. This is simple to say of the biblical preacher that he is the presenter of God's divine revelation from a man to men

God, if preachers of His Word allow Him too, will become the power source who operates in the heart of the minister's own individual personality to produce for God's purpose a persuasive spirit filled preacher whose objective is to proclaim Jesus to a lost world of people in need of spiritual conversion. They labor to teach Jesus Christ as Savior, and that Christianity is not a man-made religion, but a God ordained faith.

What is a biblical style of preaching? First, one must develop a style preaching divinely tailored to best serve each individual preacher's lifelong spiritual journey. One must love pastoring the church community and have a spirit to love God's work on earth. The pastoral experience will always lead to a spiritual relationship connecting the pastoral leader to God but also to the people. Secondly, pastoral ministry is a person committed to sharing the Word of God from pulpits to the pews and lost people outside of the walls of a church building.

Furthermore, the biblical pastoral leader is a person who view sermons as more than written words on a script, but words divinely inspired within the heart and thoughts of himself. As God's words are absorbed in preparation one's soul willingly abandons mortal thoughts in order to reach the epiphany of the awesomeness of the Lord.

T. Harwood Pattison, a noted theologian defines preaching in this way, "...the communication of divine truth with a view to persuasion..."[8] this is an adequate definition of preaching from an earlier period. It is a means of unfolding the preaching experience presented to hearers of the church community from preachers. A developed style of preaching from those proclaiming the gospel must possess that certain holy energy of divineness from God for construction of the sermon, which must be theological sound to reach an intended audience.

It is from these prospective that a proper style of preaching is compatible to one's personality. The voice is a valuable asset to the preacher; however, it is not to become the pride of the preacher to have this gift. The style of the preacher is a gift the minister acknowledges publicly. Exploring preaching styles of the New Millennials of the gospel focus on limiting some of the stresses associated with pastoral ministry. It has become common for personal, and spiritual conflicts in preaching and pastoral care leads

---

[8] Pattison Harwood T, *The Making of the Sermon: For the Class-Room and the Study*, American Baptist Publication Society, Philadelphia, 1902, p.3

to heart attacks, depression, body ailments, and even suicide. All have become prevalent among novice ministers of the gospel. Many of them abandon the gospel ministry either because they were never called by God or the pressure of ministry life is too great for them to handle. In doing so, they chose to pursue other vocations because they fear failure in areas of their preaching abilities.

However, the pastoral's lifestyle must be a spiritual constant. A lifestyle not consistent with God's biblical standards of preaching can eclipse into a messy life for one who preaches the Gospel. God's Word reveals to ministers, that, "This is a faithful saying: "If a man desires the position of a bishop, he desires a good work." (I Tim 3:1-2, NKJV).[9]

Look also to   First Timothy 3:4-7 for additional directives for preachers expressly, and ministers offering concise spiritual guidance for pastoral lifestyle, as well as a call to a life of holiness by Jesus' pastors. Social relationships must be regulated. In light of that, the Scriptures teaches, "Do not be misled: Bad company corrupts good character" (First Cor. 15:33, NIV). [10] Because, throughout the Scripture God has always held His ecclesiastical messengers in high regards as His example for people to follow. There are numerous challenges to a new generation of preachers in ministry. The purpose of the pastor leadership is to emulate the preaching and teaching of Jesus Christ. These ministers are God's human bridges on earth standing at the foot of the cross of Jesus in

[9] 1Timothy 3:1-2 New King James Version
[10] 1 Corinthians 15:33 New International Version

modern time declaring from the ancient text of the Bible the birth of Jesus, His death on the Roman cross, His burial, resurrection, and ascension.

Chapter Two: Preaching Styles from the Old Testament

The call to preach the gospel from God is that unexplainable spiritual unction, an overpowering sense of purpose within the deepest self of a person, this divine call to minister for Christ, has no real explanation. It is a call from God.

Consult with any preacher, and they will tell you ministry did not happen overnight for them. No matter what side of the earth a preacher may have come from they will testify that what they are now as pastoral leaders and preachers was a journey of mistakes, struggles, family loss, and financial crisis.

From experience, the call to preach is a call that reaches into the soul of the man of God into the unsearchable faculties of one's (inner most being) driving a person to respond and affirm through a public acknowledgement. Hebrews Chapter 11 validates, that, the only reliable and reasonable conclusion as to why one accepts God's call to Christian ministry is a simple act of faith. Reading in the epistle of Hebrews, it presents a record of men and women acting out of faith that God had divinely called and inspired them to perform the specific task of speaking His Word or leading and delivering people out of some type of crisis for His glory.

Developing a particular style in the role of biblical preaching of the twenty-first century is a challenge but worthwhile. There are deep roots anchored in the biblical text of the Bible and its galaxy of God's prophets who were seers, king, farmers and so on. Answering the Lord's call for the task of preaching in Old Testament these prophets were men who came out of, in some cases, different local settings, backgrounds, life styles, and cultures. The Old Testament pastoral leaders were the ones who led God's people as He directed them through His spoken Word to great heights for the glory of the Lord.

Nevertheless, they were recognized as physical and spiritual instruments of God. What earlier patriarchs of preaching did, they set the stage for how preaching would play a major role today and how the Word would be declared. With that in mind, Old Testament prophets shed light on styles of preaching, and gave the fundamental patterns for administering God's Word with authority.

Arnold and Beyer determined that, "Three men especially helped lay classical prophecy's foundation"[11] . In fact, the prophetic and preaching history of Israel viewed from a human perspective began with Moses, Samuel, and Elijah. They were the original preaching patriarchs of prophet leaders who laid the groundwork of preaching. At a glance, Moses, Samuel and Elijah preached and led the people of God during periods of crises and in different centuries of Israel's history.

---

[11] Arnold, Bill T. and Beyer, Bryant E. *Encountering the Old Testament,* Bakers Books, Grand Rapids, Michigan, 1999. p. 340

These men did not have the luxury of using the tools of these modern times. They presented God's message to the people in its original form. During these Old Testament periods, leaders and prophets were in its purest sense of proclaiming what God wanted them to reveal to His people. They were hermeneutical and expository preachers, who exposed and proclaimed the words God spoke to them extracting as He instructed, so their hearers could digest and then response to the message in faith.

Moses for example held two citizenships, Egyptian, and Hebrew, yet reared in the house of Pharaoh from his birth according to the biblical narrative of Exodus Chapter 2:1-15.[12] A further analysis of Moses' life reveals, for the first forty years of his life while being groom as a Hebrew, then during the same period he brought up as an Egyptian citizen. Moses killed an Egyptian and ended up fleeing from Egypt for his life. The next forty more years are what proved most beneficial. Now at eighty years old, his life falls into the hand of God's transforming power and there is a spiritual enlargement of Moses life and God lifted him up as one of the greatest prophet, leader, and lawgiver of the Old Testament.

At eighty years old Moses' years of leading four-legged sheep back and forth through the desert., unknowingly had taught him the art of leadership. It was in the desert, a wasteland that he encountered divine predestination. The day he encountered the living God in the desert plains near Horeb Exodus 3:1.[13] Meanwhile,

---

[12] Exodus 2: 1-15 King James Version
[13] Exodus 3:1 King James Version

he experienced a divine paradigm transition that transform his life, leading him to labor for God the last forty years of his life as God's prophet, leader, and lawgiver of the Israelite people. Moses' preaching style undoubtedly was robust and sometimes very charismatic in nature. One key element of a preaching style that shaped Moses was his art of either declaring or celebrating God's Word. To illustration this idea, Israel, after their deliverance from the land of Egypt with Moses as their leader experienced God's mighty hand divinely open the Red Sea and lead them across on a dry riverbed according to Exodus Chapter 15:1-21.[14] Also revealed in Exodus, Moses, following God's intervention on Israel's behalf set them free. Glimpses of celebratory preaching occurs immediately following Israel's deliverance from four hundred years of enslavement.

In Exodus 15:22-26 [15]where the tone of the celebration is silenced as the prophet and preacher Moses comes forth speaking with a voice sounding more like that of a lion and not that of a whimpering lamb because of Israel's complaining. Moses' pastoral leadership and style had nothing to do with his wittiness or education, but it was a dependency upon obeying the voice of the Lord. When spiritual tests confront ministers, learning to keep a cool head will save their ministry when those challenges arise. The above example refers to God's refusal to allow Moses to enter into the Land of Canaan. Moses should have followed God's directions

---

[14] Exodus 15:22-26
[15] Ibid

and spoken to the rock for water to come forth. Instead Moses lost his cool head and tapped the rock twice Exodus 20:7-13 for water to flow from it.[16] What is learned from this example is it is much better to follow God's instructions than for pastoral leaders to take matters into their own hands and used words of anger and hammered the rock rather than speaking God's truth as He has command.

At some point in a minister's preaching experience, learning humility will elevate God's servant leaders to great height. The pulpit has no place for folly and foolishness in the work of a Holy God. Arrogance driven by pride does not mix together. However, maintaining a divine connect with God essentially boils down to an unswerving prayer life which keeps ministers of God in good spiritual condition to be used of the Lord in His service.

It is through the Old Testament that light is shed on the first style of preaching through several roles held by prophets. They served as God's prophets and spiritual leaders of the people. They were responsible for Israel adhering to the Covenant, so that He might grant the perpetual blessings upon the children of Israel as His chosen people.

Reading over Israel's long history and her up and down relationship with God one can see the great need for a prophet. Whenever Israel rebelled and strayed from the Covenant, the prophets whom God called would bring them back into the divine Covenant through the declaration of God's Word. Arnold and Beyer

---

[16] Exodus 20: 7-13

point out, "...the prophets were not hysterical babblers...."[17] From his view of preaching God's prophets were men who spoke as God directed them. The Old Testament Prophet's messages were not outlandish or nonsense talking nor incoherent. They spoke with clarity as His mouthpiece in a time when Israel needed to hear God's Word. Secondly, Samuel the prophet who had become Israel's spokesman and mental conscious during one of the nation's volatile period in the Old Testament. This history gives contemporary ministers in the twenty-first century a view of preaching in an Old Testament format preaching styles which represents God in this generation. For instance, Samuel's prophetic messages from God to the people was a style of narrating stories. Through Samuel the *seer,* he acted out the Lord's divine revelation of Himself in extraordinary ways in order to interact with men through His prophet, leaders and preacher.

The account of Samuel's birth and call as a prophet and pastoral leader are recorded in First Samuel Chapters 1 through Chapter 3. They trace the prophet's public calling as Israel's new prophet and pastoral leader who became one of the most celebrated birth conception miracle account in the Old Testament. He rose to become one of God's greatest prophets recorded in biblical history.

Validating the validity of preachers called by God in First Samuel Chapter 3 shows that, every messenger God ever calls, has a divine intervention which takes place in their lives. J. Sidlow

---

[17] Ibid, p.342

Baxter observed, "...Samuel has few peers; and as a factor in the early growth of his nation he is equaled only by Moses... Beside this, the appearance of Samuel marks the institution of the prophetic office."[18] There are two point revealed from Baxter assertion. First, ministers can glean from Samuel the Prophet's style of preaching for one who possesses the authority of God to lead and proclaim to His people the Word of God with confidence and without fears of intimidation. It is God that sanctions the biblical minister with authority whenever they speak on His behalf. However, when messengers of God become fearful of saying what "thus saith the Lord" they relinquish their preaching authority.

Unlike the style of Moses, Samuel is the new breed who leads Israel as prophet and judge. This practice was engrained into his character from his childhood due to his mother's vow of lending him to the Lord to fulfill her commitment to God; this is the biblical recorded in First Samuel 1:28 King James Version.

These historical facts from the scripture reveal Samuel's training as a prophet. It started while he was no more that a micro-plasmic substance developing inside the womb of his mother Hannah. At his infancy and divine calling his style of preaching was a prototype for the art of preaching. Examining First Samuel 19:20, Samuel headed one of first known seminary schools for prophets as the training ground for future prophetic leaders of the Lord.[19]

---

[18] Baxter Sidlow J., *Explore The Book*, Zondervan Publishing House, Grand Rapids, Michigan, 1960, Volume Two, p 47
[19] 1 Samuel 19:20 King James Version

Training preparation for spiritual ministry is not a new concept. Its origin began early in Old Testament times. The Scriptures reveals the life of the Prophet Samuel which uncovers a style preaching that is fitting for pastoral biblical leadership and administration. Through his unique pastoral swagger, his demeanor and fearless presentation of the Word of the Lord drew Israel's leaders and the alliance of the people of God to higher standard in their relationship with Him.

Samuel as a prophet of God is represented as a personification of God. Through his authoritative type of preaching, his messages driving force focused on "what thus saith the Lord" rather than identifying with the status-quo during a time when the nation of Israel sought leadership. In fact, Arnold and Beyer observed, "The people longed for a leader who could pull the kingdom together and give them a sense of national pride and identity."[20]

This brings us to the prophet Elijah. Biblical scholars defines the name Elijah to mean, [21] "Yahweh is God" and according to I Kings chapters 17 through 18 the Bible introduced one of the boldest and charismatic prophets in the Old Testament. Up to this point of the fore mentioned chapters, preacher love styling themselves as faithful and fearless messengers of God. What ought to be remember is, Elijah was flesh and bone like any other person, and like all men

---

[20] Arnold Bill T. and Beyer Bryant E., *Encountering the Old Testament,* Baker Books, Grand Rapids, Michigan, 1999, p. 196

[21] Pfeiffer Charles F., Vos Howard F. and Rea John, *Wycliffe Bible Encyclopedia,* Volume 1, p. 517

who are human he had his strengths and weaknesses. However, Elijah had a vividly pronounced style of preaching shrouded in God's divine covering. In fact, the New Testament describes him as; Elijah was a man with a nature like ours...." (James 5:17, NKJV).[22]

His method of doing and being God's man for the hour was challenging King Ahab; Israel's most pathetic, paranoid and weakest king. Because of his weak tracts as king and leader of Israel he led the nation down the road of apostasy. In spite of Elijah's proclaiming of the Word of God, Ahab did not have the spiritual nor moral stamina to stand up against the evil and devilishness enticements of his pagan wife Queen Jezebel.

Likewise, during the time of Elijah, those living in those volatile years viewed the prophet as the contemporary preacher of his day. Also during Elijah's time in Israel's history, the people had grown defiant, disrespectful and disobedience to God. This simply reveals the unchanging nature of humanity through the history of the world. These were some of the very issues that Elijah was called by God to address using only the Word of the Lord as his method of dealing with a broken king and a backslidden nation.

Therefore, it is imperative that God's preachers stand as the conscious of God in a twenty first century culture that has become alienated from the Lord to declare His Word. Nevertheless, God has not changed in his abhorrence of sin, nor has He changed His approach to speaking and dealing with man's blatant rebellion

---

[22] James 5: 17 New King James Version

The Pastor Dilemma

against His Word. He faithfully continues to authorize faithful preachers to present His Word to a twenty first century culture that believes less and less in the Sovereign God.

Chapter Three: Biblical Preachers and Their Styles

There are three absolutes of Old Testament preaching. There is divine proclamation which is God speaking through His chosen messengers. Secondly, divine illumination, the art of imparting to the people as God works with the hearer to convict, clarify, edify, and explain. Thirdly, Divine Transformation, salvation of the lost soul back to God when they have been exposed to the light. Preaching the Word of God exposes that which is concealed in darkness to be revealed in the light.

H. Beecher Hicks, Jr. argues, "...preachers ought not to entertain too many notions about popularity, and in any case, I pity the preacher whose primary purpose is to be popular. You can't be popular and prophetic at the same time." [23] Additionally, first century preachers in the New Testament give twentieth century ministers a recorded view of preaching styles. It is an art not to be abuse by any of God's messengers. Based on the observations on Hick's views of new millennial pastors, preacher or any person called to spread the gospel, the goal is not that of building a

---

[23] Hicks, Jr., H. Beecher. *Correspondence with a Cripple from Tarsus*. Grand Rapids, Michigan: Zondervan Publishing House, 1990, 72

preaching persona that reflects a self-centered person who believes their unique talent set them apart from all other ministers. In other words, ministers of God can harm their character as a person and preacher when they project an image that says, "It's all about me!" The Bible acknowledges Jesus as a ministers' supreme model for preaching. In fact, during Jesus' first preaching engagement, He did not set out vying for popularity. It simply was not a part of His divine agenda. As revealed in Luke's gospel, Jesus said, "The Spirit of the Lord is upon me, because he hath anointed me to preach the gospel...And the eyes of all them that were in the synagogue were fastened on him...And they said, Is not this Joseph's son?" (Luke 4:18-22, KJV)[24].

The New Testament reveals narratives of Jesus calling and preparing His disciples for the preaching experience. Matthew's gospel as recorded in chapters 4:18-22 and 9:9, furnishes some examples of Jesus making disciples. He called a total of twelve men as His followers in the gospel writing. Wyclife defines the word "apostle" in Geek as, [25] "...apostolos comes from the verb apostellein, "to send" "to send forth." ...so that the agent becomes an extension of the personality and influence of the master..." This

---

[24] Luke 4:24 King James Version
[25] Pfeiffer, Charles F., Howard F. Vos, and John Rea, eds. *Wycliffe Bible Encyclopedia*. Printing, 1979 ed. Chicago: Moody Press, 1975., Volume 1, 116

included James, John, Peter and others of the apostles in the circle of Jesus.

They followed His preaching styles which characterized and shaped the way each of them would present God's Word. In fact, every, miracle, narrative, parable, prayers, test, trial, or teaching discourse of Jesus exposed His apostles to the formation of their preaching power to become better able through the aid of the Holy Spirit to proclaim Jesus' death, burial, resurrection, ascension, and imminent return.

In addition, Jesus prepared His disciples for the painful ordeal of carrying out His Word. Their individual personalities were a factor in their methodology in the art of preaching. Peter for example, was notorious for his hotheadedness. The Bible records Peter's propensity of allowing his personality to get in the way of following Jesus' directions at times. He acted as if he knew more about God's divine order than Jesus did. An example of this, Mark's gospel reveals Peter's arrogance and Jesus' rebuke of Peter shown in Mark 8:32-33. The gospel writer Matthew illuminates Peter's fears in the presence of imminent danger according to Matthew 14:30. In this instance, Peter has obeyed Jesus' command to step out of the boat onto and walk on the stormy waters of the Galileans Sea, but his humanness overpowered his spiritual confidence in Jesus in the miracle. Similarly, like all minister of the gospel we soon discover that in pastoral leadership our powerlessness is compensated in the power of Christ working in the minister's life.

Furthermore, as human beings, flaws are expected, but shaping one's character is a difficult task. This will require spending a great deal of time in prayer and meditation and with the aid of the Holy Spirit a preacher's personality gradually develops into a new spirituality that resembles the "fruit of the Spirit" recorded in the Apostle Paul's writing to the Galatians 5:22-26. As a result, the pastoral minister's ministry begins to take shape and create an image-likeness of Jesus Christ, whereas they eventually arrive as effective preachers of the gospel.

Paul explains the process of spiritually growing into the image of Christ through the active work of the Holy Spirit in the lives of gospel ministers. He says, "When I was a child, I talked like a child, I thought like a child, I reasoned like a child. When I became a man, I stopped those childish ways" (First Cor 13:11, NCV).[26] In terms of maturing as pastoral leader there are and will always be some spiritual deficiencies in the lives of preachers. They too are flawed as all humans are and no different from Jesus' apostles in the New Testament gospel and other historical writings of the Books of the Bible.

In light of those biblical characters in the Scriptures, some of them were untrained, unprepared and in many cases uneducated. Because they knew and had a personal relationship with Jesus their method of sharing His words and works began taking shape not long after His death, burial, resurrection and ascension into heaven.

---

[26] 1 Corinthians 13:11 New Century Version

In the history of the infant church, and her first century preachers of the gospel the Book of Acts records a style of preaching from the first patriarchs of New Testament pastoral leaders. For example, in Acts Chapter 2, Peter, Jesus' trusted follower is reportedly delivering the first New Testament sermon. Throughout the narrative of Acts Chapter 2, as the Scripture reveals, "Those who accepted his message were baptized, and about three thousand were added to their number that day" (Acts 2:41, NIV).[27] What does this statement mean? It means preaching styles such as Peter are the products of a spiritual trait housed within the soul and personality of regenerated ministers of the gospel.

It is from this context that New Testament preaching expanded into and throughout the first century. Jesus had taught his apostles the importance of following His example because He was the master of preaching and teaching. Reading the Gospel, narratives and parables were two of a number of methods Jesus used to mold these first century disciples. Through Jesus' three years of teaching, after His departure they shaped the art of preaching into their own God given spiritual gifts as believers to raise an army of Christian followers for Christ. The first apostles' journey of preaching commenced with the Master Preacher. It marked an evolving revolution of ministers proclaiming the divine story of Jesus' birth, death, resurrection and ascension. Adding to the idea of a growing minister is the problem of seeking popularity. Nowhere

---

[27] Acts 2:41 New International Version

in Jesus' teaching does He give lessons on the subject of becoming admired and popular by those of the world. Instead, it is just the opposite. Repeatedly in Scripture, Jesus warns His followers about the trapping of popularity. Very late into His earthly ministry according to Matthew's gospel, an argument ensued between the disciples of Jesus over the issue of "greatness" Matthew 18:1. Jesus responded to the problem with a picture lesson, He placed a small child in their company to illustrate the vital lesson of humility in order for them as His followers in Matthew 18:2-3.

To further drive home His point, evading the temptation of popularity as a tool for preaching styles, Jesus warn the apostles of the danger of taking on a world views to gain recognition like those of the "king and lords of the Gentiles" Luke 22:25-26. In other words, preachers must reframe from the notion of seeking positions of the status quo.

In the New Testament's gospels, the Apostle Peter portrait is one of Jesus prominent leaders of the inner circle ministry. Peter is described as, out spoken, strong in his conviction of personal views, and at time over bearing in what he believed. He is an example in the New Testament who reveals flaws of the all preachers in their human nature.

The Apostle Peter is vividly characterized by Walter A. Elwell and Robert W. Yarbrough in their description, "He became the Rock that Jesus said he would be"[28] therefore, for several reasons Peter possessed a unique style of preaching after close examination of his life.

The gospel records, he lives in the fishing town of Bethsaida near the Sea of Galilee in John 1:44. Similar to Old Testament prophets, location placed a vital role in styles of preaching as did in the New Testament. Peter entrepreneurship as an industrious fisherman gave him a kind of inner courage to face the harsh life as a pastoral leader. This also had a lot to do with his toughness as a sea going professional. As an angler he was quite robust in physical strength, in the gospel's presentation, sometime this strength may have cause some of the hot temperedness, and retaliatory responses which help his boldness that sometime got him in trouble in his preaching of the gospel.

This is not to say that these dispositions were carried into his preaching call. In fact, after Jesus called him as one His twelve apostles God molded Peter's character for preaching as a factor in the spiritual shaping of his pastoral ministry service.

The apostle's style of preaching correlates with his environmental, socio, religious, and theological circumstance. They were determining factors that prioritized Peter's form for preaching. However, the Scripture paints a poor picture of Peter as a candidate for preaching, but as all ministers who were ever called into the

---

[28] Elwell, Walter A., and Robert W. Yarbrough. *Encountering the New Testament: A Historical and Theological Survey.* Second ed. Grand Rapids, Michigan: Baker Academic, 1998, 2005 p. 362

gospel ministry by Jesus and the Holy Spirit, they orchestrate the approach for preaching in each individual for delivering the gospel of Jesus Christ.

A survey of Peter's first sermon as recorded in Acts Chapter 2 reveals the Apostle's bold style of preaching. It reflects his ruggedness as "the big fishermen." Peter's fearlessness in the presence of opposition was never an issue. Of course, considering Peter in this light may seem oxymoronically confusing especially given the fact that he had flatly denied knowing Jesus and any association with Him during the trial in the early morning before His death on the cross Luke 22:55-56.

Meanwhile, about fifty days after Jesus' resurrection the Apostle Peter is empowered by the Holy Spirit in Acts Chapter 2, what the Bible refers to as "Pentecostal" his bold confident preaching and pastoral leadership emerges. Throughout the remainder of his life he dedicated himself as a staunch defender of the faith in Jesus Christ. His life in the written record of God's inspired Word service as an example for preachers who follow after him. He was a biblical leader who was very human, flawed, and failed at times, but his life exemplifies the true character of a pastoral preacher of the Gospel. Herbert Lockyer argues, "Peter will ever remain a lesson to us in that he teaches us the answer to human frailty, and how the weak can become strong and the fearless can become bold..."[29]

[29] Lockyer, Herbert. *ALL THE APOSTLES OF THE BIBLE*. Grand Rapids, Michigan: Zondervan Publishing House, 1972. p.149

Peter the Apostle of Jesus was bold in his preaching style; his proclamation of presenting Jesus reveals his mastery in art of apologetics in his deliverance of God Word in these two epistles the derivative of the words *(small letters)* writings of First and Second Peter. Defend his credential and identify him as the "Apostle of Jesus Christ" in First and Second Peter in the opening introductory of Chapters 1:1 unfold who he is and his relationship to Christ and the church. As an apologist Peter was a proclaimer of God's Word, expositor of the Word, explainer of Word and as such provided a biblical philosophy to the church community in his day that were struggling to hold on to their faith in Jesus Christ due to the harsh persecution under the hand of Nero, Emperor of Rome during the period.

From these two epistles, we get a glimpse of the character of the Apostle's boldness in the face of great danger, and an enthusiastic passion of encouraging the church of his day and culture as he appeals to the moral conscience and spiritual life of the church.

Peter's style of preaching is notably unveiled through his passionate care of the church community in the closing words of the epistle of First Peter 5:18. The doxology reveals him as a man of God who has a deep passion for the call of preaching during his years of the pastoral discipline. This too, in the twenty-first century reveals to a new generation of messengers of God the shaped of a style for preaching in culture which dates back to Hebrews of the Old Testament and the early church New Testament believers into the present day culture.

41

Above all Peter the "Rock" developed into the kind of gospel minister that most twenty first century ministers can identify with. He showed a pattern for preaching in the context of one who encountered Jesus on the busy sea of coastal of Galilee. It is through Peter and those believers who had chosen to mold their philosophy of preach from the eyewitness accounts of all the followers of Jesus Christ. They were pioneers preachers who forged and gave shape to modern day pastoral caregivers, preachers, evangelist and teachers of the gospel of Jesus. It is because of these stalwart preachers of the past that today's philosophy of the gospel has developed the conversation for those seeking to become apologetics who choose to retain their spiritual authority of delivering the Word of God.

Chapter Four: A View of Preaching During the Pauline Era

At the beginning of the New Testament Church, the Apostle Peter and Apostle Paul were key figures of the apostles. They were similar to those prominent Old Testament models assimilating the great leaders and prophets like Moses and Samuel. Like them Peter and Paul dominated the preaching world building and organizing church communities as leading voices of God. During the early stages of the infant Church after the rise of Peter, the biblical pastoral shapers gives way to the Apostle Paul as the church took on new dynamics and challenges in a Grecian-Roman society. Paul the apostle was one of the most colorful organizer, builder, church planter, and powerful preacher in the history of the church.

Paul's personality styles for preaching in the early days of the first century church leaves imprints of his Christian character written in thirteen epistles of the New Testament. The author, W. Graham Scroggie observed, "...in no other man means that was equal to such a task; in other words, God made this man for this work."[30] Scroggie, in his in-depth scholarly investigation of Paul's

---

[30] Scroggie, W. Graham, *The Unfolding Drama of Redemption,* Grand Rapids, Michigan Kregel Publications 1994, Vol. 2, p 287

personality, ones immediate attention is drawn towards the apostle's styles of preaching which was overpowering, mesmerizing in an audience gripping presentation of the gospel of Jesus Christ. His assertion of Jesus' crucifixion, death, burial resurrection and ascension had little to do with his education, heritage, pedigree or citizenship. It was just the opposite. His authority in the power of preaching resulted from his belief in the Christ of the cross and the power of the infallible Word of God.

Furthermore, an inquiry into Paul's life as for as his culture being of Roman and Jewish lineage afforded him the opportunity of having the right of entry to a superior education. Scholarly Gamaliel (Acts 22:3) laid the foundation of Paul being well versed in all the cultures he would encounter throughout his preaching of the gospel ministry.

Paul's life and style of biblical preaching which is the blueprint of pastoral leadership from any writer's viewpoint, whether past or present, cannot give an exhaustive presentation of the scope of Paul's preaching power, moral convictions, intelligence and spiritual insight into the mysteries of God's Word. His style of preaching embodies a preaching from the soul. Because what is learned as one follows Paul's style of preaching is the art of persuasion that touched the lives of saints of God and sinners.

Of course, Paul loved and enjoyed preaching. Preaching should involve, first, understand human nature with a view to persuade. The pastoral leader personality must be impactful almost appealing to those he preaches too. In other words the call to preach is not something to be liked, a pastor must come to enjoy the work of preaching and pastoring the church community God has sent him to lead.

The love *"agape"* within the heart of real caring pastors produces an emotional connection between them and people in all areas of life including the lost, the hurting, those in economic dilemmas, and the whole spectrum of the mankind can relate to the preaching conversation and are drawn to the pastoral minister possessing such pastoral qualities. Knowledge of the saving power of Jesus Christ and the wondrous miraculous saving power of the Holy Spirit speaks through ministers as vehicles of delivering the Word of God.

Additionally, every generation of pastoral ministers, men of God must come to the knowledge that preaching and pastoral leadership is an art, but if the minister fails to pursue and acquire preaching skills there is an uneasiness of doing the work God has called them to do. The simplicity of preaching with authority and power from His messengers comes as a result of who He is in God and the willingness to mature emotionally, spiritually, from within. Paul instructs Timothy in his writing to, "Study to shew thyself approved unto God, a workman that needeth not to be ashamed, rightly dividing the word of truth" (II Tim 2:15, KJV).

Another fact of the pastoral leader's spiritual vocation is, God made every individual different. He gave each messenger different personalities, backgrounds, cultural rearing, and other circumstances that shaped their lives for preaching. In other words,

45

God never intended for everybody to be the same. He added diversity into his creative work in the creation of His world.

For instance, Paul, Peter, Samuel, Moses and Elijah were persons whom God called among other leaders to render spiritual leadership for His saints. Each of them in their own eras governed themselves, first as men and then as pastoral extensions of God's work. The pastoral identity continues in modern day leadership of God's Church. John B. Polhill describes Paul's early background says, "Tarsus...in having such a rule by philosophers for a time. And, that time was the period of Paul's youth." [31] In addition, scriptural references of Paul ascent to apostleship was in the hand of God working long before his Damascus Road conversion experience.

A brief survey of Roman history reveals a series of phenomenon in the life of the apostle. Paul grew up in Tarsus at a time when the Roman Empire ruled and dominated the known world. Its laws, culture, religion, economics and language dominated the then Roman World.

Under the Roman Empire, roads were constructed for military conquest, Greek became the dominate language, great philosophers were the educator of that period. Moreover, Paul was the recipient of these extraordinary times and events. It is for this purpose that Paul's unique abilities that his styles of preaching

---

[31] Polhill John B., *Paul and His Letters.* Nashville, Tennessee: B&H Publishing Group 1999, p. 8

evolved. He was located in the right time in Tarsus educational nurturing as mentioned in Acts 22:3.

The nature of Paul's style of preaching point directly to his life's world views as it relate to the place of his rearing in tutelage of a Greek and Hebrew of the City of Tarsus. These made Paul a recipient of two citizenships with the legal right to claim birthrights as belonging to Roman and Hebrew nationality. For every age period, God ordains for His people the right preacher to serve in that generation as His appointed leaders and the same is true in the twenty first century. Similarly, style of preaching that shaped the pastoral call evolved because of rapid cultural changes and challenges in Paul's era in the ancient world.

Historical observation has revealed, "Paul was never content merely to present Christianity; threats to the purity of Christian doctrine...By voice and pen he fought for purity of Christian doctrine in his day."[32] Additionally, these genre views of Paul's style of preaching were conducive with his spiritual conviction of Jesus Christ, the Church and Paul's tenacious passion for clarity when he presented the Word of God in an ungodly culture. Nonetheless, the style of preaching for twenty first century preachers are shaped and sharpen by these historical and biblical legacies that Paul left behind. Just because 2,000 more centuries and more have passed since Jesus' death, burial, resurrection, ascension,

---

[32] Cairns, Earle E., *Christianity Through the Centuries A History of the Christian Church* 1982 28th Rev. ed. Grand Rapids, Michigan: Academie Books-Zondervan Publishing House, 1982. p. 67

and the establishment of His Church it does not mean that preaching, and the problems of the biblical messenger's problems have become fewer in the twenty first century worldview, they have just become more complex.

Even though Paul laid the foundation for the style in the early stage of Christianity his biblical examples serves as a guide for modern gospel preachers. However, this does not mean that he is the primary source for twenty first century preachers to build their preaching style around. Ultimately Jesus Christ is the divine example for the paradigm of preaching. Scripture points out "Looking unto Jesus the author and finisher of our faith; who for the joy that was set before him endured the cross, despising the shame, and is set down at the right hand of the throne of God" (Heb 12:2, KJV).[33] Therefore, in a like fashion, Paul had to depend on God and the leadership of the Holy Spirit to adequately preach Jesus Christ as the living Lord.

On the other hand, what it does mean is this, Paul had relied on Christ and the Holy Spirit for proclaiming the gospel. The same criteria must be met for modern day ministers. The gospel preaching community maintained and defended the Word of God and His message as contained in His Holy Word, The Bible. Therefore, the Word of God has survived over the centuries through wars, cultural changes, and world views that reject the Bible as the Word of God and the existence of the eternal God. Notably,

---

[33] Hebrews 12:2 King James Version

Paul's intellectualism produced a style of preaching unmatched since his time. H. I. Hester maintains that, "Many unprejudiced scholars rank Paul as one of the greatest men who ever lived." [34] In addition, to Hester's presentation of Paul's timeless impression and influence on preaching in a Jewish and Roman culture, he forged the Christian faith forward with a preaching persona unmatched no other since his time period.

Therefore, the quest to replicate or duplicate Paul's style of presenting the Gospel ought not to become a pursuit and protocol in the life of ministers to be like Paul or any other minister. However, for a good method for presenting God's Word the gospel, one must investigate and examine a style of preaching suited for one's individual personality. In fact, examining Paul's life and preaching style from a biblical or historical context he far excelled in the art of preaching.

After a view of Paul's intellectual power and gifts, one can conclude that he possessed an earned place of prominence. He also was a gifted preacher who became a religious icon under harsh and antagonistic pressures in spreading the "Good News" of Jesus' birth, death, burial, resurrection, ascension and the return. As a realist, Paul was equipped spiritually for the task of preaching Jesus the risen Christ in his day. This has already been confirmed in a prior discussion regarding his training under the tutelage of Gamaliel, and conversion on the Damascus Road, giving him the edge, he needed

---

[34] Hester, H. I., *The Heart of the New Testament,* Broadman Press 1980 34th ed. Nashville, Tennessee. p. 253

for presenting the gospel to Jewish, Roman, Gentile and pagan cultures.

In other words, though Paul had lived and preached during different cultural setting, in an ancient oriental time he accomplished awesome feats of spreading the gospel without modern technical tools of the twenty first century. Yet without the technological tools of electronics, the mass-media, or computers of today's modern age it was his preaching of the good news of the good tiding of Jesus Christ which dominated the landscape through his powerful and persuasive epistle, preaching of an unwavering gospel. Christianity became the dominate faith in a Roman culture in his day because of his preaching.

Studying the Apostle Paul is a gigantic undertaking in the twenty first century, however, we are led to believe his preaching is powerful and persuasive. Meanwhile, Roy L. Smith points out, "…Paul admitted very candidly that he was not a great success as a public speaker (I Corinthians 2:1), but even his enemies had to admit that he was an effective letter writer (II Corinthians 10:10…."[35]

Smith also states, "…the converted Pharisee has become the world's greatest thinker and evangelist."[36] In other words, preachers of the gospel of Christ do not have the same abilities, yet this should not become a hindrance. In fact, Paul was as serious about defending the faith as he was a spiritually serious man. He also had a real

---

[35] Smith, Roy L. *Know Your Bible Series Study Number Eight,* New York – Nashville, Abingdon-Cokesbury 1944 p. 4
[36] Ibid, p. 63

passion for spreading the gospel of Jesus Christ, and it was his desire for all preachers to give their best service for the glory of God. The Apostle Paul scriptural guidance for written conversation in many of his epistles is a spiritual aid for preachers to read in order to work on their own preaching styles from a biblical perspective. God has imparted spiritual gifts in the lives of every minister that enabled and equipped them for His glory. Paul instructed his young protégé of the gospel to, "Let no man despise thy youth; but be thou an example of the believers, in word, in conversation, in charity, in spirit, in faith, in purity." [37]

Building a spiritual persona, Paul's writings in the epistles are essential and the vital source in an ongoing process of becoming biblical preachers with the purposeful intent of guiding Christian communities for continued growth or the work of preaching the gospel to the lost. Which means personality is everything; in light of the fact that, Paul used what God had given him as a minister and apostles.

Therefore, like the early Christian apostle of Christ who concerns were to emulate themselves in His pattern of preaching and pastoral style and not worry about assimilating other preachers. But what did matter to Paul was the fact that he was getting the work of the Kingdom of God done through his own biblical style of preaching the gospel for the glory of God and not his own. More

---

[37] First Timothy 4:12, KJV: Criswell, W. A., The Criswell Study Bible 3rd ed. Nashville, Camden New York, Nelson Publishers, 1979,

importantly, in the modern culture of pastoral ministers the goal is to be more like the original pattern for preaching Jesus left with His disciples, and the type of pastoral leadership style presented in the history records of the Bible.

Chapter Five: Biblical Preaching for a New Culture

The question of where did a biblical style of preaching originate? Earle E. Cairns argues, "...the foci of the Book of Acts are the resurrection of Jesus Christ, as the subject of apostolic preaching...."[38] In fact, the opening chapter of the Book of Acts is a continuation of Luke's Gospel which bear his name. Noted in Acts Chapters One and Two, several miraculous events had occurred leading up to what has become labeled as biblical preaching. First, Jesus' final instruction to the disciple regarding where they were to begin the preaching campaign (Acts 1:1-8). Secondly, there is the empowering of the Holy Spirit the Greek language He is Paracletos), defined as, "That which searches, knows, speaks, testifies...."[39] Thirdly, within the same context, the arrival of the Holy Spirit (Acts 2:1-4). Finally, the infancy of a biblical preaching style (Acts 2:5-41). It is within these contexts of Acts that a form of biblical preaching emerges in the life of the early church. The preaching

---

[38] Cairns, Earle E. *Christianity Through the Centuries a History of the Christian Church*. 1982 28th Rev. ed. Grand Rapids, Michigan: Academie Books-Zondervan Publishing House, 1982., p 56
[39] Bancroft, Emery H. *Christian Theology Systematic and Biblical*. 2nd Rev. ed. Grand Rapids, Michigan: Zondervan Publishing House 1961, p 158

discourse reveals Peter proclaiming the gospel to a Jewish audience who had rejected the idea that Jesus was the Savior who would come to save them.

Profoundly, the personality of people is altered by the person of the Holy Spirit as seen in the life of Peter who became a bold and willing preacher of Christ. He is simply being himself, sharing the gospel with people, from all walks of life in a Roman and Judaic culture in the known world of that period. Peter's presentation of the life, death, burial and resurrection of Jesus Christ argument was the fulfillment proclaimed by Old Testament prophets who had foreseen the revelation of the coming of Jesus Christ.

In fact, Merrill C. Tenney biblical survey of early preaching of those first preachers observed that, "…Unlike modern preaching, which is usually either the logical development of some topic… the apostolic preaching was a narration of the life of Jesus, with a defense of his resurrection…"[40] whereas, we are therefore given a written visual perspective on apostolic preaching.

In other words, the first Christian sermon of the New Testament preached by the Apostle Peter gives us some perception of the style of biblical preaching declared by our first century prognosticator of the gospel. Now, this does not imply that modern day preachers should not prepare for the preaching event, the supposition is this, early preaching was a total and complete unction

---

[40] For further investigation, refer too Tenney, Merrill, C., *New Testament Survey Revised,* 2nd Rev. ed. Grand Rapids, Michigan: WM B. EERDMANS PUBLISHING COMPANY, 1961. p. 240

of the Holy Spirit acting and influencing preachers like Peter to proclaim the gospel in the manner they did. The art of a biblical style of preaching focuses exclusively on the written Word of God because it is the only true source of real truth expose from the biblical text. Noting the Christian church first recorded verbal sermon in Acts 2, it should be noted that a pluralist worldview does not appear in Peter's message, instead, he used one source for conveying the message of God to the church which were given as narratives of Old Testament historical events as a means of persuasion to convince his hearers that Jesus Christ was crucified and rose from the dead revealing Him as the promised Messiah.

Therefore, examining the biblical text for a design for molding pastor-preachers for the leadership role of guiding the church community involves adhering to the inerrant Word of God. In light of all of Jesus' training His apostle's which entailed three years of learning from the Master Himself. In other words they attended the original school for a style for preaching. It was from Jesus that they learned the power of His infallibility and through Him they could proceed faithfully as preachers with a complete confidence in the trustworthiness of the Word of God. In addition, as preachers, one must be mindful that attempting or contemplating the use of religious views or beliefs alien to the Holy Bible teaching would certainly invalidate and misrepresent preaching the gospel of Jesus Christ.

Historically, narrative style of preaching offers an in-depth look into the preaching of biblical style preaching. Narratives give readers a glimpse of the historical sojourners of God as patriarchs of faith. The people who wrote the poetical writings of Psalms, the parables of the Old and New Testament. These miracles and the historical events of the Book of Acts contain one the most profound revelations of biblical preaching in the Scripture. In the Acts account of early church preaching all the apostles had only one key story to unfold which was the death burial and resurrection of Jesus Christ.

In examining Jesus' leaders, it is discovered that each biblical character possessed a style of proclamation unique to his personality and as God's representative his gift was best suited for God's purpose in the Scripture. In fact, narrative preaching is much more than telling a story. It is a technique employed by early preachers of the first century church and those of twenty first century ministers who familiarized themselves with a wide range of biblical texts that helped shape them into who they became as prognosticators. In addition, critical study of renowned preachers and their sermons as John Bunyan, John Wesley, Charles Haddon Spurgeon and Gardener C. Taylor reveals their commitment to biblical hermeneutics and homiletics one comes to understand the importance shaping through preaching the pastor-preachers' character.

The preacher's character makes them who they are and what they have become. The Apostle Paul recognized this when writing, "For I am the least of the apostles, that am not meet to be called an apostle, because I persecuted the church of God. But by the grace of God I am what I am: and his grace which was bestowed upon me was not in vain; but I laboured more abundantly than they all: yet not I, but the grace of God which was with me" (First Cor. 15:9-10, KJV).[41] Now, here is a biblical patriarch demonstrating personal experience of the necessity of good character born out of pain, poverty, persecution, preaching, and praise that molded him into what God had called him to be.

Analyzing any number of Paul's writings, one discovers in those narrative how his experiences molded his character and changed his life. Paul's preaching began at a time when the name of Jesus was not popular to preach about. This unpopularity led to an anti-Jesus movement clashing with Jewish religious authorities and the Roman establishment of the times. In fact, persecution of the early church escalated because of what the apostles preaching and teaching was about. Paul was ushered into the center of the struggle not long after his conversion in Acts Chapter 9 during his Damascus Road experience of meeting face to face with the risen Christ.

Meanwhile, Paul's life was reshaped for the new faith's philosophies and its new etymological ideological paths for communicating the gospel to the world. The character of a biblical style of pastors and preacher-teachers stay diligently and consciously aware that the role they have undertaken as God leaders for His church are still relevant for the twenty-first century church community. Marva J. Dawn and Eugene H. Peterson point out, "...pastors have been told that they're not pastors but counselors and

---

[41] 1 Corinthians 15:9-10 King James Version

people who run churches."[42] In other words, in pastoral ministry style of biblical preaching it can never allow it defining relegated by world standards. In the first place, Paul confirms the importance of communicating the art of preaching from the biblical perspective when he wrote, "For I am not ashamed of the gospel of Christ: for it is the power of God unto salvation to everyone that believeth; to the Jew first, and also to the Greek" (Rom 1:16, KJV).[43]

As ministers of the gospel preaching is the catalyst in the scheme of building confidence in one's ability of presenting the Gospel of Jesus Christ. Unless God's church leader's character has a theological centered focus of biblical truths, they become no more than pulpit puppets. Pastors leading a church in the twenty-first century are faced with many challenges and it is imperative of them that they stand firm in the biblical teaching of the Scripture. The Scripture admonishes, "Wherefore take unto you the whole armour of God, that ye may be able to withstand in the evil day, and having done all, to stand" (Eph 6:13, KJV).[44]

The Scripture determines the character of preachers. Woven into the nature of the Lord's immutable attributes, it stands that the nature of pastoral preaching means God Himself administrates His servants and shapes them to His will and purpose. Ministers are the possessions of God who speak for Him in plain language, readily

---

[42] Dawn, Marva, J., Peterson, Eugene, H., *The Unnecessary Pastor Rediscovering the Call,* William Eerdmans Publishing Company Grand Rapids, Michigan 2000, p. 61
[43] Romans 1:16 King James Version
[44] Ephesians 6:13 King James Version

understood and palatable by hearers. Paul's writing to the Corinthian Church said, "My message and my preaching were not with wise and persuasive words, but with a demonstration of the Spirit's power, 5 so that your faith might not rest on men's wisdom, but on God's power" (First Cor. 2:4-5, NIV). [45]

Secondly, etymology of the preacher's words and thoughts should be cultivated in the inspired Word of God communicating with those in search of God's truth in such a way that those void and blind to the ways and Word of the Lord can receive clarity and understanding from the preached word. For example, the Book of Acts Chapter 8 records the narrative of an Ethiopian eunuch needing clarity regarding a section of scripture concealing the identity of Jesus, His sacrificial death, and redemption work of salvation too the lost. The text reveals that, Philip was instructed to join himself to this eunuch's chariot and unveiled the meaning of an Old Testament prophecy that stated, "...He was led as a sheep to the slaughter; and like a lamb dumb before his shearer, so opened he not his mouth:" (Acts 8:32, KJV).[46] What happened in this passage? The preacher's words came alive as he unveiled God's written revelation to the Ethiopian and with the aid of the Holy Spirit Philip used common language to explain and expose the mystery of the written Word the eunuch held in his possession.

---

[45] 1 Corinthians 2:4--5 New International Version
[46] Acts 8:32 King James Version

In the study of theology it deals with a major problem *"hamartiology"* which deals with the doctrine of sin and man's guilt before a righteous God. Emery H. Bancroft argues, "Sin is a reality and not and illusion…Missing the Mark of the Divine Standard"[47] Every preacher and every person are the recipients of a fallen sinful nature and through Jesus sacrificial death for sin on the cross of Calvary He is the remedy and prescription for man's flawed personality.

It is because of humanity's fallen sin natures that old background eventually catches up with what happened in the past. However, with God and through His grace it is possible to counter some negative flaws of a passed life. In order to do so, as an example, if Paul's ministry was too having the impact in the church community during his time and world culture, he learned not to fear the possibility of his passed becoming exposed. What he did to deal with bad marks of his history was to place it in God's care and work at the idea that had covered the imperfections of the past. You can never pastor with the anxiety of the past barking at your heels.

First, the Book of Acts 7:58 and Acts 8:1 reveals Paul also known as Saul of Tarsus, stood holding the coats. Jewish religious persecutors stoned and execution deacon Stephen to death who was a saint of God. In fact, Saul is giving consent to the whole process. He secured letters to have believers put to death. He acknowledged

---

[47] Bancroft, Emery H. *Christian Theology: Systematic and Biblical.* 2nd Revised Ed. 1976 ed. Grand Rapids, Michigan: Zondervan Publishing House, 1929. p. 213, 218

his unworthiness but found salvation on the road of Damascus. He experienced the pain of progression that molded his life as a preacher of Christ.

As preachers who enter into the work of preaching and pastoral ministry probably should know that one of life's most challenging ordeals for ministers of the gospel of Jesus Christ is the paradigm shift of breaking away from world culture and transforming ones-self into spiritual servants of God as He had intended for His preachers to be. To get a handle on the reason for biblical style of pastoral-preaching purpose, those who do so have the awesome task of imparting spiritual truth to the Christian Community of believers.

Meanwhile, ecclesiastical ministers of the Word of God must reshape and retrain both language and speech becoming more like the representatives of Jesus Christ. Talking beyond the level one's understanding is a disadvantage and more than likely a misconception of what it means to become more like the person of Jesus.

The pastoral leader in spite of flaws in their lives will need to "walk the walk and talk the talk" this can be achieved in and through the help of the Holy Spirit, because He is the *Parakaleo* the believer's helper and "Advocate "who walks along side" in and through Him that all things are made possible. In fact the Scripture points out and gives great insight to the matters of flaws as Paul says, "No temptation has seized you except what is common to man. And God is faithful; he will not let you be tempted beyond what you can bear. But when you are tempted, he will also provide a way out so that you can stand up under it" (First Cor. 10:13, NIV).[48]

There are a few approaches one may think about when contemplating reconstructing how molding their lives around the reality of the risen Christ can become a joy to do and pleasing to God. Because for the pastoral leader, preaching is what God has called every one of them to do. Take for example Paul's call to ministry. His life went through a transforming period as can be seen in Acts Chapter 9 which gives some detailed accounts regarding Paul transformation. He became a true advocate of preaching and pastoral leadership.

Acts 9:1-2 reveals the person known as Saul of Tarsus as a strict Jewish religious follower of the Mosaic Law. He had a notorious hatred of the Christian faith and those who followed Christ. He had no reservations about arresting known Christians and sending them to a horrific death for many who openly believed or taught other about the life, death, burial, resurrection, ascension and eminent return of Jesus Christ.

Saul who would later becomes known as Paul; his transformation would be an extraordinary episode in his life on the Christian journey. Acts 9:3-4 give the account of that life changing encounter toward conversion and reshaping of his life in the service of the Lord for preaching and pastoral care of the saints of God. First steps of spiritual transformation for preaching service, Saul came

---

[48] 1 Corinthians 10:13 New International Version

face to face with a decision which he had to make as the light shined down from heaven and enveloped him and forcefully prostrated him onto the ground faced down. He heard for himself, none other than the voice of Jesus Himself. (And then, that most important prevailing question of all that comes to the preachers in their call to ministry, ("What Lord do you want me to do?) as Paul had asked "Who art thou, Lord? And the Lord said, I am Jesus whom thou persecutest: it is hard for thee to kick against the pricks" (Acts 9:5, KJV). [49] And then, the Scripture said, "And he trembling and astonished said, Lord, what wilt thou have me to do? And the Lord said unto him, Arise, and go into the city, and it shall be told thee what thou must do" (Acts 9:6, KJV).[50]

Secondly, what does this means; no preacher can ever preach a compromised gospel. There is no negotiating of the Word of God. That being said, Jesus the Savior of the soul as presented in the Scripture is the Authenticator of all preachers who are called into biblical pastoral leadership and it's preaching in the Christian ministry.

As already asserted earlier in the text regarding the culture, pastoral leaders are expected to lead the church community of the twenty first century despite an ever-growing resistance to Christianity. Preachers and pastors face many challenges of an anti-Jesus twenty-first century culture that would rather not have any form of Christian faith. Hitchens outlandish attack on religion again

---

[49] Acts 9:5 King James Version
[50] Ibid

states, "People seem to be lying on the opinion polls as well. They claim to go to church in much larger number than they actually do (there aren't enough churches in this country to hold the hordes who boost of attending), and they seem to believe in Satan and in the Virgin Birth than in the theory of evolution"[51]

Furthermore, Hitchens and other nonbelievers are precisely the reason why preachers must develop and assert the fundamental basics of biblical of preaching. This applies especially to those involved in the role of pastoral leadership. There is a stern warning given in the Scripture regarding antagonist attacks on the body of Christ. The warning from the Scripture state, "Preach the word; be instant in season, out of season; reprove, rebuke, exhort with all longsuffering and doctrine. For the time will come when they will not endure sound doctrine; but after their own lusts shall they heap to themselves teachers, having itching ears;" (II Tim 4:2-3, KJV).[52]

Unlike the apostle Saul and his experience in the call to ministry, in the twenty-first century there are people who do not experience the kind of conversion he experienced. The remaining verses of the narrative illustrate the feared Saul of Tarsus' gradual transformation from sinner to a saint and lastly the too the Man of God. Accordingly, the Book of Acts reveals Saul's call to ministry, "But the Lord said unto him, go thy way: for he is a chosen vessel

[51] Hitchens, Christopher *god is not Great: How Religion Poisons Everything*, Twelve New York, NY, 2007, p. 284
[52] 2 Timothy 4:2-3 King James Version

unto me, to bear my name before the Gentiles, and kings, and the children of Israel:"[53]

Therefore, the minister must labor more diligently as spiritual combatants in warfare for Christ and His Kingdom in order to reach souls for the Kingdom of God. How does the life of the gospel ministers mirror that of biblical preachers of first century church leaders? It is the style of preaching presentation of modern day pastors and those gifted with the gospel not presenting foreign or superficial texts of spiritual truths. Their mirroring must reflect the writing of the Word of God. This is an area of the gospel which cannot be disregarded.

Bearing in mind, this same Paul, also called Saul in the Acts chapter 9 account of his life's preaching story was ordained of God to preach Jesus' birth, death, burial, resurrection, and ascension. The biblical instruction observes, "Now then we are ambassadors for Christ..."[54]

In the King James Version this means, pastor who labor in the Gospel are called to present a biblical style of preaching and pastoral leadership method. As flawed as preachers are in human nature they are privileged to be called ambassador of Jesus Christ.

Paul reveals the flawed personalities of humanity. Throughout Scripture, the preaching community notes they are fallen creatures because of sin. Paul recognized fallacy early in the

---

[53] Acts 9:15, King James Version
[54] Corinthians 5:20, King James Version

nature of humanity. He says, "For all have sin and come short of the glory of God"[55] whereas Paul amplifies the "The wages of sin is death, but the gift of God is eternal life through Jesus Christ."[56]

The fact is, God has always used imperfect people to accomplish His divine will. In the Book of Genesis 12:12-20 Abraham convinces his wife Sarah to lie and deceive the Pharaoh of Egypt that she was his sister. Genesis Chapter 27 records the narrative of Jacob's thievery in stealing the birthright and blessing from his brother Esau. In the biblical account of Second Samuel Chapter 11:1-21 reports King David's love affair with Bathsheba, an adulterous act which led to conspiracy of a murderous plot that cause the death of Uriah the husband of Bathsheba.

These examples show how flawed humanity is and the preacher is no exception. He, like all of humankind is in a fallen state and not immune from the effect and power of sin. However, Paul in response to the dilemma regarding the sin nature recognized God's redemptive work in the souls of those who accept His call to salvation and then God's call to preach the Gospel says, "What a wretched man I am! Who will rescue me from this body of death? Thanks be to God — through Jesus Christ our Lord."[57]

In other word, there is not a preacher living or dead of homogeneous nature who can count themselves worthy of the title of perfection in God's gospel ministry. Instead, preaching is a

---

[55] Romans 3:23, King James Version
[56] Romans 6:23, King James Version
[57] Romans 7:24-25, New International Version

privilege and not an entitlement or badge of perfection since there has been only one true preacher of perfection who is Jesus Christ. As a result, because of His perfection preacher of His Gospel possess a perfect pattern for shaping their ministry for service to God.

The Pastor Dilemma

Chapter Six: The Mental Dilemma

Pastors engaged in the work of pastoral leadership face many challenges as God's leaders in church communities, they must endure with hardships which come along with their divine calling from God. They are by the nature pastoral care giver having the awesome responsibility to answer to God for being the spiritual nurturers of God's saints. This obligation reaches not only within the confines of the local church community, but they also have the responsibility of being the local caregiver for non church goers. In doing so, this provides encouragement among other communities and at the same time it leaves pastors vulnerable to the negativities that come with the preaching territory. It is important that they have a clear understanding of their role as a biblical preacher and pastor of the Gospel of Jesus Christ.

Mollette, Glenn W. Mollette, argues, "People in small communities know the pastor. Even if they do not attend his church, his face and name become familiar to the community at large."[58] Agreeably, Mollette's argument is well founded. Because there is

---

[58] Mollette, Glenn W. Church Growth 101: A Church Growth Guidebook for Ministers and Laity. Newburgh, Indiana: Newburgh Press 2012 p.19

no way pastors can effectively have an impact on the church and community without taking an active role in the life actives of people. In a twenty-first culture motivated by worldviews, the reputation of the pastoral leader is always under scrutiny as they mix among those of the local community. The eyes of those having no sympathy for the church nor its leader sometime create reasons to give the local church and its pastoral leaders a black eye. Additionally, the Old Testament's biblical prophet Jeremiah reveals, "As for me, I have not hastened from being a pastor to follow thee: neither have I desired the woeful day; thou knowest: that which came out of my lips was right before thee" (Jer. 17:16, KJV).[59]

Ray C. Stedman argues, "…You don't make yourself into a spiritual man; nobody does. The words you need to hear are the words that Jesus said to His disciples: 'Follow me.' "[60]

That is to says, the eyes of the world monitors a pastor's lifestyle. Therefore Jesus living daily in the life of His leaders provide them power to live exceptional lives as Christian pastors the Holy Spirit who aid them in dealing with trials of the world. This is necessary if they are to work as spiritual caregivers in local churches where they have been called to serve. Paul reminded those Christian elders in Ephesus during his departing farewell address say, "Keep watch over yourselves and all the flock of which the Holy Spirit has

---

[59] Jeremiah17:16 King James Version
[60] Stedman, Ray C., and Denney D. James. *God's Loving Word: Exploring the Gospel of John.* Grand Rapids, Michigan: Discovery House Publishers 1993. p. 60

made you overseers. Be shepherds of the church of God, which he bought with his own blood...."[61]

For the twenty-first century pastoral leader, the possibility of whether the office of pastoral leadership will be challenged and that challenge will not be a matter of if those test will come, but rather pastors are always confronted with the proverbial when. Can pastors avoid conflicts among church members? Do they have the capacity to avoid certain attacks on pastoral leadership and preaching? Answers to these questions are best answered in the Scripture.

Rehashing through the following verses in Acts Chapter 20 verses 28-31 one discovers God's enemies seek every opportunity to infiltrate a church for giving her a black eye. Paul contends after departing from the elders of the Ephesus assembly that those holding opposites views on the subject of Christian faith would come and attack the church again. Judaism would once again try persuading gentile Christians to adhere to the Mosaic Law to become a part of the Christian community.

This was a serious problem in the Apostle Paul's day, and churches and her pastoral leaders today face an array of anti-biblical and erroneous teachings that demand preaching from the biblical context. Pastors therefore must overcome the stigmata of firefighters on their way to put out church fires. The real test of their mode of preaching has to do with a life testimony. For the twenty-first century church keeping a right course as followers of Jesus Christ

---

[61] Acts 20:28-31, New International Version

the preacher will face the difficulties of being able to stand strong in the flames of burning fiery ovens and never cringing at the entrances of lion's dens.

Cleophus J. LaRue and his Indian preaching colleague in India focus on the modern day dilemma of preaching experience in the twenty-first century church era both observed, "Anyone who is at all attentive to the present church scene must be aware that in every denominational tradition new forms of congregational life and new challenges to many long-established church practices are emerging. The signs of change are visible in all area of church life… Many a young pastor has fell into difficulty trying to move a traditional along too hurriedly"[62]

Agreeably, preaching and churches struggle with identity. The church and many of her leaders have fallen into potholes of trendiness. In fact, if Jesus Christ were here in this century bodily His words of "woes" would fit perfectly into this present age. Emulating the person of Jesus Christ from the preacher's message drives more worldliness into the minds the unsaved. The pulpit where God's sacred Word is supposed to take center stage and in these days the agenda resembles unholy worship rather than real worship in the house of God. No pastoral leader should ever be branded as fashion maker, dressing to be seen and not heard, addicted to one fad after another. This is not to say that the preacher

---

[62] LaRue, Cleophus J. *I Believe I'll Testify: The Art of African American Preaching* Westminster John Knox Press, 2011 p. 38

is to be a sloppy dresser rather they should clad themselves in a way that says to the hearers that, "I'm here on Kingdom business."

Therefore as preachers, the world will test the validity of the pastoral minster calling. For instance, when the first century disciple began their preaching and pastoral ministry the world was not confused about who they were and who they represented. "Now when they saw the boldness of Peter and John, and perceived that they were unlearned and ignorant men, they marveled; and they took knowledge of them, that they had been with Jesus."[63] Upon reading this narrative of Peter and John's encounter with a man who was lame from birth and miraculously his ability to walk was regained. The disciples commanded him to get up and the lame man stood up and walked because of the power and the authority of Jesus' name. This certainly identified them as ministers of Jesus Christ.

The dilemma of preaching and pastoring in a twenty first century culture has weakened some churches in an organized system so that some churches look nothing like the church Jesus had in mind, or what he described and empowered in the New Testament. Church nowadays have less identifiable label that make it difficult to know what they are. In many ministries of the new age religions they advocate none-Trinitarian believes, but operates under the guise of Para-Ministries. Yet, these same ministries do not believe in the existence of God the Father, God the Son and God the Holy Spirit are certainly functioning under a false pre-tense of preaching

---

[63] Acts 4:13, King James Version

as commanded by Jesus Christ in His "Great Commission" that instructs the Gospel be delivered according to the Gospel of Matthew 28:19-20.

However, the biblical preacher greatest test in this ecclesiological dilemma will face challenges. It is not whether the traditional church will survive, but will the pastoral preacher continue a faithful presentation of God's Word. Passionate preachers in their roles as pastoral leaders are keenly aware of the many rapid changes in modern culture. These changes are reflected in various passages of Scripture found in the gospels, historical writings of the Book of Acts and the epistles of New Testament authors.

Paul the apostle for one, gave a charge concerning the role of pastoral leadership and preaching of an early period and for every gospel minister for all time to come, says, "Preach the word; be instant in season, out of season; reprove, rebuke, exhort with all longsuffering and doctrine. For the time will come when they will not endure sound doctrine; but after their own lusts shall they heap to themselves teachers, having itching ears; And they shall turn away their ears from the truth, and shall be turned unto fables."[64]

In fact, the whole of Paul's argument in Second Timothy Chapter 2 mirrors tests pastoral leadership encountered who stand on the premise that God's Word is the authority of heaven. Persons preaching the Word of God must not become mere storytellers, but

---

[64] II Timothy 4:2-4 King James Version

the medium that evoke an awareness of the consciousness of God with author in the body of Christ in a church community. Here is where the real test really meets the road. That is to say, when the preacher or Pastoral leader must preach to a hostile crowd of people who resents the preacher and are quite content to be left alone in their sinful cultural lifestyles.

At this point, either pastor learns to trust God to strengthen them by His trustworthy Word, or physically or mentally collapse and fall apart under the tremendous pressure of stress. Bear in mind that pastors are not exempt from mental paralysis that drains their spiritual vitality to a point that then become impotent to the work of pastoral service.

Rev. Mark H. Creech Christian Post Columnist reports, "Rev. Teddy Parker Jr., 42, pastor of Bibb Mount Zion Baptist Church in Macon, Georgia, discovered by his wife in the driveway of their home, dead from a self-inflicted gun-shot wound. [1] Ed Montgomery, 49, a pastor at Full Gospel Christian Assemblies International Church, Hazel Crest, Illinois, takes his own life in front of his son, after grieving the death of his wife who had died a year earlier from a brain aneurysm. [2] Isaac Hunter, 36, founder and pastor of Summit Church in Orlando, Florida, admits to an affair that leads to his resignation, and while suffering from a troubled marriage he ends it all by killing himself. [3]"[65]

---

[65] Christian Post, *www.christianpost.com/news/pastors-mental-illness-and-suicide*, December 2013, Web. 06 December,2015

In fact, reading Creech's report he gives credence to his argument through his own struggle with this dangerous malady which plaque pastors and preachers suffering in secret. In like manner, Creech expose a feeling of inadequacy in his own life as a man and preacher can happen in the best and strongest person. Furthermore, there are examples of Old Testament and the New Testament revealing the pressure of feeling failure can lead anyone into a downward spiral. Pastors are not superhuman nor are they super spiritually exempt from falling into this very dark place.

Mental deficiency among pastors remains one of the leading causes associated with ministers abandoning their pastoral ministry and vocational preaching post. In light of Creech's revelation of pastoral mental illness and pastoral suicide, the trend affects ministers during the prime of life among denominational lines. The problem of depression is nothing new the bible points to several spiritual patriarchs who when through this emotion bout of stress such as, Elijah, I Kings 19:4, Jonah, Jonah 3:4, and Job, Job 3:1-12. These trends have deep-seated spiritual bearings in pastoral communities. One particular underlying culprit leading to pastoral burnout, nervous breakdowns, and suicide are churches operating using world philosophy and modern day cultural ideologies push pastors into that dark place of depression.

Based on Creech's observation and personal experience with mental illness, one may observe that the ministers in his post reveal an age factor. Moreover, this raises some prevailing questions of pastors and suicidal tendencies. Can some of the cause of ministers' depression be a result of going against the grain of God's Word?

Of course, there are many passages of Scripture which give ministers of the gospel spiritual guidelines and spiritual protocol for pastoral conduct regarding spiritual, ethical and moral directions for clergy behavior. The Bible points to First Timothy 3:1-8, Titus 1:5-9, and Acts 20:28 as New Testament examples to keep the preacher in tone with actions regarding how to keep a sound mine in their walk with God.

Dawn and Peterson argue "...They want a pastor they can follow so they want have to bother with following Jesus anymore...[66]" In this discover clearly pastors find themselves under gratuitous stress because the church community place responsibility on them that could be carried out by laity leadership. Most churches filling vacant pulpits with pastor they do not intend to follow. The person God has placed in the church as over-seer. They are called upon to be the pastor when some politician needs a boost from the church community. They rarely receive monetary compensation for their service while some churches fill its coffers with the proceeds of the membership only to boast about large bank accounts. In the word of the Prophet Jeremiah, God said, "And I will give you

[66] Dawn,Marva J., Peterson, Eugene H. *The Unnecessary Pastor: Rediscovering the Call,* Grand Rapid, Michigan / Cambridge U. K.: William B. Eerdmans Publishing Company, 2000. p 4

pastors according to mine heart, which shall feed you with knowledge and understanding."[67]

The pastor's finance is another cause of depression. They have the right to take care of their families as the church membership. Sadly, those who are suppose to look out for welfare of the pastor, some lay leaders have a nasty habit of waving the carrot but never sharing. A pastor's finance like any marriage if that is the case place tremendous strain on family.

T. A. Prickett make four important points in reference to the pastors says, "The pastor needs also to give attention to care of his physical life...pastor's social life is very important...It is not easy to have a major social life as a preacher...The pastor's family is of extreme importance...Divorce is a real problem in today's world, and the pastor's family is not exempt from this pressure."[68] As the Prophet Jeremiah pointed out regard the type of pastor give to His church they are gifts given to the church for the purpose of declaring God's truths.

However, laboring as the church's spiritual caregiver consumes a large amount of a pastor's daily routine. The schedule is often interrupted by telephone call from sick members, a call to come to the hospital or bereavement that may call for a trip to a grieving family in the middle of the night. Then there is the most important task of all, sermon preparation.

---

[67] Jeremiah 3:15, King James Version

[68] Prickett, T. A. *We Preach Christ: The Man, The Method, The Message.* Bloomington, Indiana. AuthorHouse 2004 p. 7-8

Preaching is what God has called the man of God to do and preaching they must do! They cannot preach without a sermon which means some important obligations will be left undone or neglected. The work comes at a high cost. The family, because of pastors' hectic schedules cause stress on their family life.

This is true for nearly all pastors in the twenty-first century than ever before. They burnout long before they reach their wisdom stride. Suicide is one of those taboos rarely addressed in the pastoral community and the reasons are numerous. An important fact, preachers are human with human feeling and are not immune to a world of challenges and tests. God never created them to fill the role of divine human nor has He called pastor as a one person "do it all" nor are they to position themselves to go through life as pontificators.

Further, maintaining good mental health pastors as well as every day Christian should let other people know they can have stress taking them to a dark place in their lives. But the good news it this Jesus Christ has granted the believer soundness of mind. All one needs to do is trust Him when He says, "Come unto me, all ye that labour and are heavy laden, and I will give you rest. Take my yoke upon you, and learn of me; for I am meek and lowly in heart: and ye shall find rest unto your souls. For my yoke is easy, and my burden is light." [69] Depression happens, therefore, Christ is the divine answer to the disease. However, having one close friend to

---

[69] Matthew 11:28-30, King James Version

share with in confidence is a step in the right direction to cope with this silent killer of self destruction of human life.

Dr. Glenn W. Mollette explains "Depression is no respecter of person..."[70] In like manner; pastors cannot separate humanness from life's experiences. The malady of depression touches the lives of those in all professions including ministers of the gospel. In fact, a pastor is the one person who must work diligently at maintaining a healthy mental state. Mollette advises, "... lawn work and exercise...joining a gym ..." [71] Agreeably, beating depression requires some self effort and self-intervention to the problems to deal with personal issues encountered by pastoral ministers. A few things a pastor can do to combat stress and depression are taking out time for leisure with the family, going to the mall, or just taking time to get away from church for a time is good mental therapy. Seeking professional counseling is not as shameful as one might be lead to believe, the shame would be doing nothing compared to allowing the problem to ruin a precious life. That being said, Mollette advice "We have to trust our stress and headaches to God."[72] Mollette gives his readers some of the best advice regarding mental health. It is a means of helping ministers come to grips with the pressures of pastoring in the twenty-first century church community. Coming from a pastoral prospective, reading and listening to this kind of

[70] Mollette, Glenn W. Church Growth 101: *A Church Growth Guidebook for Ministers and Laity*, Newburgh, Indiana: Newburgh Press, 2012 pgs. 37-39
[71] Ibid
[72] Ibid

good wisdom is an encouragement for pastors who find themselves in a state of depression or contemplating suicide having faith in the power of God and His Word is to the minister's advantage.

The Pastor Dilemma

Chapter Seven: Biblically Sound Conflict Resolution

One of the fallacies of pastoring is conflict in the body of Christ and without any doubt those conflicts will raise its ugly head within the church community. This validates the old idiom that says "sooner or later trouble will come." Conflicts have always challenged the church community from her inception.

Dennis Bickers explains "Conflict is inevitable in ministry regardless of the size of the church. Its denominational polity, its theology, or the expertise of the church staff and lay leaders have nothing to do with the matter. Churches are made up of people, and whenever people are involved, there is the potential for conflict. It is certain that conflict will arise in every ministry, but what is uncertain is when it will occur and what it will be about..."[73] However, as holy as the church is suppose to be, history has proven time and time again that church and ministering in a church regardless of it demographics it is certainly no rose garden or walk in the park, so to speak.

Though there were conflicts in the church the gospel spread steadily. One conflict threatening the existence of the church

---

[73] Bickers, Dennis. *The Healthy Pastor: Easing the Pressures of Ministry.* Kansas City: Beacon Hill Press, 2010. p 86

appears in the New Testament in Acts Chapter 6. It revealed a disagreement between two groups. The passage in question, "And in those days, when the number of the disciples was multiplied, there arose a murmuring of the Grecians against the Hebrews, because their widows were neglected in the daily ministration. Then the twelve called the multitude of the disciples unto them, and said, It is not reason that we should leave the word of God, and serve tables."[74] The passage reveals tension in the church community of the first church which originated from complaints levied by the Greek Christians against the Hebrews Christian for neglecting to take care of their widow's daily food and financial needs.

Acts chapter 6 gives the postmodern day church kind of a window into the church's early history. Through the written Word conflict is exposed. The situation is so intense that the apostles were lead to remedying the conflict. Had the disagreement continued to fester one could see that this one incident could have overthrown the church causing it to disband and dissolve into a circular organization.

In the twenty-first century church the answers to resolving conflicts are still matters that require prayer, and the leadership of the Holy Spirit. God was in the decision making of the early church. However, many church leaders make the mistake of leaping into church fight without first assessing the cause, and history behind the

---

[74] Acts 6:1-2, King James Version

problem. In all probability the pastoral ministry takes the brunt end of the infighting.

Pastors who develop a biblical style for preaching similar to those demonstrated of the first century church leaders will see conflict as an opportunity for church growth. Resolving the tension in the church's first business meeting Acts Chapter 6 exposed a method of resolving church conflict that was to take a wise and prayerful approach. They saw that they could not serve tables and remain faith to the preaching of the gospel. The apostles assembled the church, and then allowed the church membership to choose qualified men to serve the needs of ailing church widows. Here is where good pastoral insight takes place. The problem is there which could be detrimental to the life of the church or a conflict most often become an avenue for church growth. The latter proved to be the most effective, which was prayer that brought about an even stronger church body and free the apostles to do the task they were called to do, which was to preach as Jesus had commanded them to do.

The role of pastoral leadership seeks the guidance of God through prayer. This is not a novel approach to any of the issues confronted by the church community. In fact, Jesus made many promises to His church as He ministered among the disciples for three and a half year. Two of the most prophetically profound promises are found in His words of authority baptized with His assurance that "...I will build my church; and the gates of hell shall not prevail against it.[75] "...and, lo, I am with you alway, even unto the end of the world. Amen."[76]

A major problem that most pastoral leaders face is developing a preaching style that will meet conflict cautiously. Many pastors who are either new to the field of pastoring or veteran pastors coming to a new church where there is open conflict are faced with the question of what should. Many of these churches render an uneasy feeling, with patience and a loving spirit. There are some matters within many church communities that are best left alone, especially the old ones. There is an old saying which has no etymological history that say, "Let sleeping dogs lie" [77]

However, the biblical pastor will never escape conflict. It is one of the hard facts associated with ministry leadership. No amount of seminary training or circular psychology can prepare the minister for the approaching storms of squabbles. The Scripture is the only tool that addresses these spiritual issues. Jesus' instructions to His disciples at the conclusion of His earthly ministry concluded by telling pastoral leaders in the church's postmodern era in regards to His mandate He instructions are, "As you go, preach this message: The kingdom of heaven is near."[78]

Therefore the pastoral leader should never abandon the ministry unless they are unable to handle the pressure of all the

---

[75] Matthew 16:18, King James Version
[76] Ibid
[77] *Let sleeping dogs lie* (etymology history unknown)
[78] Mark 10:7, New International Version

responsibilities that goes alone with biblical preaching because conflict will come. Be thankful to God for the blessing. Yet, conflict among church leaders do clash from time to time. What must be done to head of a brewing conflict pastor remain faith to the preaching agenda as prescribed by the Scripture. Paul the gallant preacher the Judeo and Gentile Christian faith charged all pastoral preachers to, "Preach the word; be instant in season, out of season; reprove, rebuke, exhort with all longsuffering and doctrine."[79]

God did not give the biblical pastor commands to run at the sign of impending storm, "For God hath not given us the spirit of fear; but of power, and of love, and of a sound mind."[80] If fact some pastoral have invested an enormous amount of time and energy developing a style of preaching to become defenders of the Gospel of Jesus Christ.

Aside from conflicts encountered within and without the church community. There are other kinds of conflicts caused by a minister's through their own personal misconduct. In regards to the pastor/preacher's lifestyle, ministers and pastors are often singled out because of their unique roles in society and church community. The pastoral lifestyles apply to every minister of the gospel even though the individual may not hold the title pastor, a great responsibility of public reputation rest on them in the local church community and their families.

---

[79] II Timothy 4:2, King James Version
[80] II Timothy 1:7, King James Version

Furthermore, pastors as well as the laity must maintain a lifestyle consistent with biblical principles as a part of the biblical style of preaching. Within the pattern set forth in pastoral leadership however, the Apostle Paul offers clear spiritual instructions from the Scripture says, "This is a true saying, If a man desire the office of a bishop, he desireth a good work. A bishop then must be blameless, the husband of one wife, vigilant, sober, of good behaviour, given to hospitality, apt to teach; Not given to wine, no striker, not greedy of filthy lucre; but patient, not a brawler, not covetous; One that ruleth well his own house, having his children in subjection with all gravity; (For if a man know not how to rule his own house, how shall he take care of the church of God?) Not a novice, lest being lifted up with pride he fall into the condemnation of the devil. Moreover he must have a good report of them which are without; lest he fall into reproach and the snare of the devil."[81]

Here the infallible Word of God not only gives the qualification for the pastoral ministry, but within the framework of these same scriptures are found the biblical instructions that will keep ministers personal and spiritual lifestyle in synchronized with the written Word. If the minister could only abide by these guiding scriptures the less like they will need to deal with the personal conflicts that often hamper their ministries.

They must also be cautious about the kind of social involvement with associating ministers and friends. Because,

---

[81] 1 Timothy 3:1-7, King James Version

Scripture teaches, "Do not be misled: Bad company corrupts good character"[82] There are many gifted ministers who have lost their pulpits, and ministries because of bad behavior, but many of them have fallen by the wayside and gone back out into the world. It is of grave importance that pastors have the resolve to maintain their focus as representatives of God while dealing life issues and the headaches of leading the church community.

The key to faithfully preaching the gospel is the art of learning to be you and not practicing how to become like someone else. An often error for novice preachers is imitating other preachers. Mimicking their pastors or seminary mentors may be fine for learning and grounding purposes, but at some point, in their ministry an apprentice will need to work and discover their own person in the gospel ministry. Because every preacher is flesh, blood and bone riddle with flaws, whereas, to some ministers may not bother them, but these same flaws can potentially cause a short lived ministry for a novice minister.

Therefore, a minster must become resolute to move towards taking serious steps at discovering one's own selfness as a preacher and pastoral leader. Yet, acquiring and accomplishing these goals might be lengthy for some, but the development the of your specific style will be uniquely you that will differentiate your styles of pastoral leadership from anyone else.

---

[82] 1 Corinthians 15:33, New International Version

The Pastor Dilemma

Chapter Eight: The Forming of Biblical Pastoral Leadership

James W. Thompson in his insightful work, *Pastoral Ministry according to Paul: A Biblical Vision* says "My purpose is to move beyond the focus on the roles of the minister and the how-to literature of ministry in order to determine the ultimate aims of our work."[83] The pastor/preacher who fails to examine the biblical role of preaching and the role of pastoral leadership are destined to become pulpit puppets in church leadership. Postmodern churches in of the twenty-first century fashion themselves as elite, popular, mega are the churches which govern power and control over pastoral leadership and the pulpit. In many instances, pastors that don't have the theological stamina to confront these issues are sought out by church committees to fulfill their unscriptural church agenda.

Present day churches have a worldview concept of what a pastoral leader ought to be. It believes it deserves a show for worship in Sunday's services that is geared towards excitement. Does the first-century church address the egotism of some of these twenty-first century misguided churches? The Scripture says, "But God

---

[83] Thompson, James W. *Pastoral Ministry according to Paul: A Biblical Vision.* Grand Rapids, Michigan: Bakers Academic, 2006. p. 11

chose the foolish things of the world to shame the wise, and he chose the weak things of the world to shame the strong. He chose what the world thinks is unimportant and what the world looks down on and thinks is nothing in order to destroy what the world thinks is important. God did this so that no one can brag in his presence" (First Corinthians 1:27-30, New Century Version NCV).

For a style of biblical pastoring and biblical leading, the new millennial church Christ centeredness eludes the membership. In many cases, rather than becoming a member of a generally small church there are a number of people who opt to join large mega churches so as to get lost in the multitude. Some members choose to remain numbers on the church money giving list without ever building a Christ, pastor, and church relationship. Some never experience pastoral care during crisis, such as bereavement, lost of employment, family issues, teenage interacting only to mention a few. Missing in the whole relationship is connecting and staying connected to the source. Included in the spiritual connection are pastors, laity leaders, and lay members of a local church community. In one of Jesus" teaching session with His followers He taught, "I am the Real Vine and my Father is the Farmer. He cuts off every branch of me that doesn't bear grapes. And every branch that is grape-bearing he prunes back so it will bear even more. You are already pruned back by the message I have spoken. Live in me. Make your home in me just as I do in you. In the same way that a branch can't bear grapes by itself but only by being joined to the vine, you can't bear fruit unless you are joined with me."[84]

The biblically connected pastors are often out of the loop so to speak when they are not fashionable dressing pastor, the celebrity type, or high profiled. They are deemed as out of step with time by pop culture generation. Thompson argues, "Paul's goal is the transformation of the community that will turn from self-centeredness to a corporate existence shaped primarily by the love exhibited by the self-denial of Jesus..."[85] Additionally, as twenty-first century pastors strive to shape God's biblical style approach to pastoral leadership in an volatile and biblical unstable cultural environment, it is the true church community that seeks stable pastors who follow the mandated spiritual teaching of the Church's founder and keeper Jesus Christ.

Paul, for example, believed transforming churches were possible in the early days of the infant church writing in a small letter written to Titus he says, "To Titus, mine own son after the common faith: Grace, mercy, and peace, from God the Father and the Lord Jesus Christ our Saviour. For this cause left I thee in Crete, that thou shouldest set in order the things that are wanting, and ordain elders in every city, as I had appointed thee..." (Titus 1:1-5, KJV)." In other words, the church out of necessity the church must prayerfully

---

[84] Peterson, Eugene H. THE Message: The Bible in Contemporary Language. Seattle, Washington. 2002 P C Biblesoft v 5
[85] Thompson, James W. *Pastoral Ministry according to Paul: A Biblical Vision*. Grand Rapids, Michigan: Bakers Academic, 2006. p. 59

search for qualified spiritual pastoral leaders with a love Jesus Christ, and heart filled with compassion the church and the willingness to share with the lost the birth, death, burial, and resurrection of Jesus.

In a twenty-first century culture, can a biblical style of preaching for pastoral leadership be shape based on a New Testament generation theology? Reexamining the qualifications set forth in the Epistles of First Timothy 3:1-7, and the Epistle of Titus in its entirety, discovered in these writings no room is left for neophyte or those seeking to become celebrities as a means of entertaining the saints. Harold Willmington profoundly reveals in his outlines on the Epistle of Titus regarding biblical leadership styling:

"ELDERS FOR THE CHURCH (1)

1:1-4 From Paul, God's servant, to Titus, Paul's child. Paul greeted Titus, who like Timothy was his "child" in the faith (see exposition on 1 Tim 1:1-2).[86]

He reminded him of the glorious gospel they both proclaimed, which God had "promised . . . before the world began" (see exposition on Eph 1:1-6).[87]

1:5-9 "Select shepherds who meet the standards." Paul had left Titus in Crete to bring order to new churches. He was to appoint

---

[86] 1 Timothy 1:1-2 King James Version
[87] Ephesians 1:1-6 King James Version

godly leaders for each church. Concerning the requirements for such leaders (1:6-9), see exposition on 1 Tim 3:1-13.[88]

1:10-16 "Here's why we need them." The appointment of elders was urgent because false teachers — especially Judaizers — were trying to lead believers astray. Titus should soundly rebuke such deceivers. As the context suggests, "everything is pure to those whose hearts are pure" (1:15) refers to Mosaic dietary laws, not morals in general (see Matt 15:11; Acts 10:15; Rom 14:14). Paul had strong words for those who "claim they know God" but in fact do not (1:16; see 2 Tim 3:5). Christ condemned such hypocrites as well (see Matt 7:21-23; 23).

Titus 1:10-16; Titus 2:1-10; Titus 2:11-15; Titus 3:1-8; Titus 3:9-11; Titus 3:12-15

MINISTRY IN THE CHURCH (2-3)

2:1-10 Tips for junior and senior saints. Older men should be serious and sensible. Older women should be godly role models for younger women. Younger men should be self-controlled (2:1-6). The pastor himself should be an example in both walk and talk (2:7-8). Servants can elevate Christ by obeying their masters (2:9-10).

2:11-15 What to do while awaiting that blessed hope. Paul reminded Titus of the good news of grace, showing how grace should affect everyday life (2:11-14). He urged him to boldly declare this truth (2:15). A proper understanding of grace will

---

[88] 1 Timothy 3:1-13 King James Version

produce good works and Spirit-controlled living as we await Christ's return. See exposition on Rom 1:1-7 and on Eph 2:1-10.

3:1-8 Why Christians should be good citizens. Christians should be models of good citizenship and good character (3:1-2, 8) because by God's grace and by the presence of his indwelling Holy Spirit (3:4-7) we have been saved and are being saved from our sinful, selfish human nature (3:3).

3:9-11 Avoid both debates and debaters. Arguments such as those promoted by the Judaizers are useless and should be avoided. Those who promote such things should be admonished not to do so. If they fail to repent, they should be excommunicated (compare exposition on the following passages: Matt 18:15-20; 1 Cor 5:1-8; 2 Thess 3:6-15).

3:12-15 "Hope to see you in Nilopolis soon!" Paul stressed once more that God's grace should motivate good works. He told Titus he was sending someone to replace him for a while in Crete so that he could join Paul in Nicopolis."[89] Accordingly, based on the reliability of the infallible Word of God, restoration of God's church is the ultimate goal for a style of leadership that is scripturally fundamental to the church of Jesus. However, pastors set the tone for change if the paradigm of a Christian cultural is to occur within in a time when worldview bombards the church community. The health and shaped pastoral leaders must maintain a God-mindedness

---

[89] Willmington, Harold. Willmington's Bible Handbook, Wheaton, Illinois: Tyndale House Publisher's, 1997.--- P C Biblesoft, 1988-2006. V. 5.

to hold on to God's Word which declares His promise of never forsaking His church.

Pastoral ministry come with a certain amount of pressures that affect the process of building a ministry that is conducive to forming and atmosphere of godliness in the pastoral/preaching arena.

In the framework of pastoral ministry, pastors and overseer must see themselves as vital assets to the church, chosen by God as gifts to be its pastoral leaders. In other words, change does not take place unless the pastoral-leader gets close-up and intimately personal with the membership. In fact, the Apostle Peter and author of First Peter reminds spiritual leaders especially shepherds and overseers of churches, that, "The elders who are among you I exhort, I who am a fellow elder and a witness of the sufferings of Christ, and also a partaker of the glory that will be revealed: Shepherd the flock of God which is among you, serving as overseers, not by compulsion but willingly, not for dishonest gain but eagerly; nor as being lords over those entrusted to you, but being examples to the flock; and when the Chief Shepherd appears, you will receive the crown of glory that does not fade away" (First Peter 5:1-4, NKJV).[90]

Adding to that, a cultural Christian shaping of the church community those in charge of exhibiting Christian view is primarily the pastor's responsibility. Jesus in the course of teaching the disciples used parabolic and metaphorical language to teach an

---

[90] 1 Peter 5:1-4 New King James Version

importance lesson for transforming the lives of people. In the Gospel He says, "...I am the good shepherd: the good shepherd giveth his life for the sheep. But he that is an hireling, and not the shepherd, whose own the sheep are not, seeth the wolf coming, and leaveth the sheep, and fleeth: and the wolf catcheth them, and scattered the sheep. The hireling fleeth, because he is an hireling, and careth not for the sheep. I am the good shepherd, and know my sheep, and am known of mine..." (John 10:11-14, KJV).[91]

Therefore, imperative to shaping pastoral consciousness for shaping and reforming a congregation into Christ-like mind, pastoral leader prayer life must be focused to God's spiritual mandated agenda. Those who pastors or have a biblical calling to the ministry, regardless of their intelligence, astuteness or education, the power of preaching emerges not out of wittiness but a consistent prayer life. An Old Testament patriarch named Jacob discovered the power of prayer in his struggle with the angel of the Lord one night according to (Gen 32:26).

In other words, the pastor who communicates with God in prayer gives him divine access to God's throne of grace. Prayer allows God to hear and answer the pleas of pastor's personal matters and church leadership issues.

However, a disciplined prayer life strengthens pastors spiritually for the immoral challenges of the twenty first century. Why a consistent prayer is is important? The Christian pioneers of

---

[91] John 10: 11-14 King James Version

pastoral leadership penned the Scriptures centuries ago for the pastoral ministry to continue as the biblical standard for ministry today. The challenges of living within the realms of godliness, runs much deeper in postmodern times. One such pastoral pioneer of first-century like Paul said, "Pray without ceasing. In everything give thanks: for this is the will of God in Christ Jesus concerning you" (1 Thess 5:17-18, KJV).[92]

Many pastors in the course of their ministry experience anxiety; a sense of being overwhelmed in postmodern times due to a free-living culture of worldviews practices which has infiltrated the church community and this worldview way of life think very little of the consequences of sin in the world.

However, Christian pastors should not abandon the ministry to partake in worldly sins to fill up those avoid some issues of life. Instead, God offers biblical avenues of spiritual directions and strengthens for pastors in times of fear, frustration, and those feeling of viewing pastoral work as unimportant. The imperativeness of prayer is commander by Jesus, the model of all pastoral ministries says, "Men ought always prayer" (Luke 18:1, KJV). In essence, Jesus' commanded the disciples those whom He left in charge of His church were to have a consistent lifestyle of prayer.

The true of the matter, in today's culture of ungodliness many good pastors are abandoning their posts as pastoral leaders and the major reason stems from a lack of conversing with God in

---

[92] 1 Thessalonians 5: 17-18 King James Version

prayer. Paul while in prison shared powerful the enticing the love of the world when he penned the sad news, "…Demas hath forsaken me, having loved this present world, and is departed…" (Second Tim 4:10, KJV).

Bickers argue, "…the issue of friends, and that is when the wrong people want to be friends with the pastor. They may cause more stress then the problem of not having friends"[93]

Therefore, instead of changing the church from a culture worldviews, the pastor who chooses friendship over pastorship of church members could fall prey to the enticements of the world. The Apostle Peter as has been already seen in First Peter 5:1-4 revealed the type of pastors God has called to lead.

Pastoral isolation falls into the category of biblical shaping for pastoral leadership. God often than none sends His leaders through times of purging such as trials, tests and temptations as a means of preparation for the task of leadership. Health issues, economy challenges, family pressures, and the like remind pastoral leaders of his dependency upon God. However, it is these exercises of hardships that build a deeper personal relationship with God who is the great equalizer of any problem for the pastoral ministry. The Scripture says, "And we know that all things work together for good to them that love God, to them who are the called according to his purpose" (Rom 8:28, KJV).[94]

---

[93] Bickers, Dennis. The Healthy Pastor: Easing the Pressures of Ministry. Kansas City: Beacon Hill Press, 2010, p. 71
[94] Romans 8:28 King James Version

Meanwhile, God called pastors as His unique servants to be defenders of the Gospel. Their pastoral calling requires visibility in church ministry, and community involvement as an active participant in local community programs. Nonetheless, pastors must come to grips with the reality that God created all people from the same earthen material, and His ministers are no exception. This means pastors should strive to keep their bodies, minds, and spirits in fit condition because, when the body breaks down from over-work and stress what good are they to the people of God when serious health issues prevents the effectiveness of pulpit ministry?

The Pastor Dilemma

Chapter Nine: Building a Style of Preaching in Pastoral Ethics

John Maxwell defines "ethics" as, "An ethical dilemma can be defined as an undesirable or unpleasant choice relating to a moral principle or practices..." [95] This definition indicates that an individual must personally examine the moral behavior regarding ethics or distinguish the difference between that which is wrong or right. In turn, ethics is a means of discovering how one should base decision-making on spiritual and moral basics to come to a conclusion of proper conduct as a Christian pastor.

Making unethical choices such as lying and cheating only escalate further frustrations in the role of pastoral ministry. An imperative of pastoral ministry is the responsibility of adhering to the principles of following the "Golden Rule" which reads, "Therefore all things whatsoever ye would that men should do to you, do ye even so to them: for this is the law and the prophets" (Matt 7:12, KJV). [96] In addition, teachings from other biblical text reveal how pastor can greatly reduce scandals later as they mature

---

[95] Maxwell, John. *There's No Such Thing as "Business Ethics": There's Only One Rule for Making Decisions.* United States of America: Center Street a division of Hachette Group, 2003. p. 5
[96] Matthew 7:21 King James Version

in their pastoral roles as they become wiser in making minor and major decisions.

Practicing pastoral ethics should not have to come out of a book or a classroom lecture. God has interwoven it into the fabric of human nature. In fact, ethic is a behavior taught in Christian's homes to children early in life by parents and they most often prefer using the wisdom of the Scripture writing, "Train up a child in the way he should go: and when he is old, he will not depart from it" (Proverbs 22:6, KJV).[97]

Other areas of biblical style for preaching addresses the issues unethical ways in which some leaders use their calling as a tool to manipulate their followers for the purpose living extravagant lifestyles and fail to teach the followers to follow Jesus. However, all pastors do not conform to these unethical and manipulative agendas. Actuality, Jesus taught against such unethical practices of hypocrisy to His followers and those teaching resonate in Scripture today as He had said, "…The scribes and the Pharisees sit in Moses' seat: All therefore whatsoever they bid you observe, that observe and do; but do not ye after their works: for they say, and do not…." (Matthew 23:2-3, KJV).[98] In other words, a failure to abide by Jesus' clear teaching of the Scripture regarding what is ethically, morally, and spiritually right is a slippery downward slope to damaging the pastoral image.

---

[97] Proverbs 22:6 King James Version
[98] Matthew 23:2-3 King James Version

Essential Christian ethics as pastoral is learning the importance of growing into the larger understanding of ethical choices. Wrong choices will often place pastors in a position which they may never recover. In fact two of the wrong choices are paramount and worth noting. Caught in an uncompromised position with the opposite sex, sexual impropriety and misappropriation of money, embezzling or stealing. It does not matter how they are labeled, these two cause scandal, place a black mark on the church community and mar the reputations of ministers and impacts the church he services in a negative way. Pastoral ethics is everything, and the Scripture validates it over and over again.

For instances, the Scripture teaches, "But the path of the just is as the shining light, that shineth more and more unto the perfect day. The way of the wicked is as darkness: they know not at what they stumble" (Proverbs 4:18-19, KJV). [99]

1. The completed documentation of the biblical Commandments God outlines His standards of ethical behavior, Exodus 20:1-17.

2. Jesus gives of Beatitudes of Christians ethics taught in Matthew 5:3-12.

3. Paul explanatory epistle underscores Christian ethics as loving and doing the right thing, Romans 13:9-10.

4. Ultimately Jesus Christ is the Light and supreme example of Christian ethics, according to John 8:12.

---

[99] Proverbs 4: 18-19 King James Version

The Pastor Dilemma

Therefore, it is up to the individual pastor and preacher to shape a style of pastoral leadership not to imitate worldly ethics but the kind of ethics that is taken from the blueprint of God's Word.

Along these lines of the Golden Rule, it is this guiding principle which determines the actions of pastoral life and leadership. In doing so, not only do pastors gain the trust of others, but also his method of making right choices for the good of all concerned forms the biblical style of preaching for pastoral leadership shaping.

Maxell points out, "a person of responsibility can trust himself to choose the thing over the easy thing..."[100] The author's views are right on point. Decision making is never easy, but blaming other people for mistakes which are sometimes are made even with the best intentions, it is not Christlike to play the blame game. That's life! Being pastor mistakes happens, however, the first thing to do when things have gone totally wrong. Look within yourself and take responsibility for your actions. Pray and ask God to intervene. The Scripture teaches, "Ask, and it shall be given you; seek, and ye shall find; knock, and it shall be opened unto you: For every one that asketh receiveth; and he that seeketh findeth; and to him that knocketh it shall be opened" (Matt 7:7-8, KJV). [101]

Furthermore, ministers must look outside of themselves for an answer to problems, and then look to God as the only spiritual means they will have of not allowing many great opportunities for

[100] Ibid p. 93
[101] Matthew 7: 7-8 King James Version

preaching and pastoral care. God is a pastor's only source of pursuing and achieving a successful role in pastoral ministry in the twenty-first century. Pastors who recognize and work on some of the weaker areas in decision making will begin to identify some of the stronger points in his life.

Then again, becoming aware of certain limitations can keep them from being taken advantaged of in unscrupulous business situations. The Apostle Paul defense of his pastoral ethics, wrote, "Let a man so account of us, as of the ministers of Christ, and stewards of the mysteries of God. Moreover it is required in stewards, that a man be found faithful" (1 Corinthians 4:1-2, KJV).[102] The fact is, pastors are to be vigilant and keenly awareness of his accountable to God, therefore, He has entrusted to care for His church and be example of Christian ethics.

Henlee H. Barnette argues, "The supreme quest of the Christian is the kingdom of God and his righteousness (Matt. 6:23). In the Scriptures righteousness has a threefold meaning: stereological (God's righteousness as deliverance or salvation); ethical (God's righteousness as a norm of conduct) eschatological (God's righteousness as the achievement of his purpose in history). Jesus conceives of righteousness in ethical terms as life in harmony with the will of God"[103]

---

[102] 1 Corinthians 4:1-2 King James Version
[103] Barnette, Henlee H. *Introducing Christian Ethics.* Nashville, Tennessee: Broadman Press, 1962. p. 48

In Addition Barnette observed, "...Paul's ethics is Christo-centric... "in Christ" (en Christo), an intimate relation of the Christian with the Lord (Ro. 16:3,9; 1 Cor. 1:30; 2 Cor. 5:17 Gal. 3:28; Col. 4:7; Phil. 4:1 1 Thess. 3:8). This is not a mystical relation, but not the kind which absorbs the person into nothingness. Rather, it is a practical mysticism which denotes belonging to Christ and behaving in mind and deed like him."[104]

Oden provided some food for thought in saying, "Change does not occur without pain..."[105] adding to the point of pastoral ethics, pastoral leaders are physical living example of what it means to live as living examples of the life and walk of Jesus Christ. They should live Christian lifestyles that are pleasing to God. But how painful is change in a culture where anything goes?

Like all believers, members of the cleric community are bombarded with temptations from any number of mediums, whether it comes from an unrestrained appetite of unchecked bad habits, an undisciplined life style, television media, or the worldwide web. Any temptation that is allowed to remain will desensitize and cause callosity of the moral nature which is the goal of Satan to keep leaders of God as carnal as possible. The Scripture is like a mirror in its ability to always bring the reflection of the past to the forefront of living for God in spite of the spiritual growing pains.

---

[104] Ibid p. 69

[105] Oden, Thomas C. Pastoral Theology: Essentials of Ministry. New York, NY: HaperCollins Publishers, 1983. p. 237

In fact, the Holy writ according to Paul's writing in First Corinthians 10:1-6 reveals painful episodes in the life of God's people in Old Testament. According to Paul writing to the Corinthian Church, he write a word picture revealing one of Israel's most horrendous life experiences when they felt the wrath of the Lord due to bad choices of rebelling against the will of God in the Wilderness. Yet, the writer says in spite of all the spiritual chaos the recorded Scripture exists bring to the attention of the modern-day church community and leaders that, "Now all these things happened unto them for ensamples: and they are written for our admonition...." (First Cor. 10:11, KJV).[106] Further, applicable to the twenty-first century culture have not heeded these examples.

Though the Apostle Paul speaks the Corinthian Church Community from a first Christian century prospective of the churches growing pains and its multitudes of spiritual problems, there is much insight for the twenty-first century pastoral leaders should consider. The unheeded examples mention in the Corinthian text above ought to serve as a warning to not only the church community but, also to the pastoral preaching population as well.

Those in pastoral from the biblical perspective, they are given a high spiritual and moral responsibility they must protect with an enormous degree of tenacity. Not being judgmental of ministers' reputation, pastors and lay-ministers have suffered irreversible harm to themselves because of unethical indiscretions.

---

[106] 1 Corinthians 10:11 King James Version

Sadly, clergy in the course of the pastoral work have lost their focus after they have spent large number of years building a good pastoral relationship with and in the church community only to lose it all due to a lustful appetite for worldly pleasures or careless in how they attend to the pastoral duties. For instant, carelessly visiting women who are sick or convalescing in the home or hospital alone. This is an area of pastoral ministry that it is better and wise for the pastor to give an advance notice of a specific day and time visiting the sick person in the home or hospital will take place. Along with that, pastors should have their wife if married or another person to accompany in the visitations.

Then, there is the question of money, the pastor my keep their hands of the churches money. They should pay attention that the only money they handle is their personal salaries, and as a biblical principle they are not money-grabbers. In the C clause of First Tim 3:3 for pastoral qualification Paul writes, "…not greedy of filthy lucre…" he writes this because, he knew that pastoring and money gotten wrongfully by a pastor was another one of the devil's tools to ruin the character of the minister. The Scripture is full of examples of what will happen when God's people and more especially His servant-pastor fall prey to the money snare.

Then too, as a part of pastoral ministry, when the church's pastor is in need of some financial assistance they should not sink to the level of perpetrating side gimmicks, unsavory business deals or thing of that nature. They must learn to depend of God and trust Him in faith for all their needs.

Paul's writing in the context of First Corinthian Chapter 10 regarding the immoral behavior of Israel in the Old Testament supported his argument by show them that, "Nevertheless, God was not pleased with the great majority of them, for they were overthrown and strewn down along [the ground] in the wilderness. Now these things are examples (warnings and admonitions) for us not to desire or crave or covet or lust after evil and carnal things as they did" (First Corinthians 10:5-6, AMP). [107]

And so, pastoral ethics must be keenly observed and practiced by pastoral leaders. The salaries of a majority of pastor are never what it should be for the workload of pastoring God's people, but the Epistle of Philippians 4:19 makes it clear, "But my God shall supply all your need according to his riches in glory by Christ Jesus." In closing this session, the church has ethical and moral responsibility of providing for pastors and the families monetarily.

The Scriptures are written for the church's spiritual guidance and regarding the pastoral leader's economy well-being and financial support. God says in His inspired written Word, "Let the elders that rule well be counted worthy of double honour, especially they who labour in the word and doctrine .For the scripture saith, Thou shalt not muzzle the ox that treadeth out the corn. And, The labourer is worthy of his reward" (First Tim. 5:17-18 KJV).[108] "If we have sown spiritual seed among you, is it too much if we reap a

---

[107] 1 Corinthians 10: 5-6 Amplified Bible Version
[108] 1 Timothy 5:17-18 King James Version

The Pastor Dilemma

material harvest from you? If others have this right of support from you, shouldn't we have it all the more? (First Cor. 9:11-12, NIV).[109] Barnette argues, "For every ethical consideration has its connection with "the whole Idea of God."

---

[109] 1 Corinthians 9:11-12 King James Version

Appendix

Appendix of Sermon Questionnaires Based on Paul's Preaching

Pre-questionnaire based on a series of sermon survey on Paul's epistle letters written during the first century of the Christian Church and their impact on the first century church, and how they spiritually typify the twenty-first century church community.

The sermon surveys were evaluated by four membership responders of the Zion Spring Missionary Baptist Church, of Okolona, Mississippi with age groups ranging from 30 years old with young families, others age ranging between their 40's and 60 year old age range. These fellow church attendees listened and observed attentively to a series of sermons relating to biblical style of preaching as a pastoral leadership tool based on the Apostle Paul's messages to the first-century church community.

They were asked to write a short review in one or two short sentences whether the message was informative, helpful and what spiritual impact these sermons had on them spiritually, personally and their church. Each observer was instructed to give their fair and honest critic regarding the biblical text preached or taught.

Pre-questionnaires based on Paul's letters to the Corinthian Church:

1. Did the sermon regarding the importance pastoring and leadership impact the church?

2. Did the sermon based on the Apostle Paul's message to the early church address the spiritual needs of today's church?

3. In your observations, how could the sermon benefit church communities in a positive way?

4. Could the sermons easily become an inspirational tool for reaching none church goers?

5. Was the sermon overall beneficial to all age groups for your church setting?

6. What challenges were presented to the church that would transform your church into better witnesses for Christ?

7. Was there enough emphasis given in the message for improving the leadership roles in your church?

Post- Questionnaires of responders:

Sunday January 10, 2016

Text: First Corinthians 10:9-13

Subject: God Want Put No More on You Then You Can Bear

I.   Planning for Temptation

II.   God's Purpose for Your Test

III.   God's Will Help You Prevail in Your Temptation

Sunday: January 17, 2016

Text: Second Corinthians 12:7-9

Subject: When Stuff Isn't Going Your Way, You Can Count On God

I.   When Stuff Isn't Going Your Way, During Life's Tests

II.   When Stuff Isn't Going Your Way, You Can Count on God Grace

III.   When Stuff Isn't Going Your Way, You Can Have Victory in God.

First Responder:

Question One: Did the sermon regarding the importance pastoring and leadership impact the church? States, "The sermon on Paul's message to the church then opened hearts and minds to the need of pastoring and leadership in the Church

First Responder, Question Two: Did the sermon based on the Apostle Paul's message to the early church address the spiritual needs of today's church? Argues, "Yes, Just as the message helped in the early church, the message is just as essential to the spiritual needs of today's church. The message directed as well as encouraged the people at that time. The message is just as powerful now."

First Responder, Question Three: In your observations, how could the sermon benefit church communities in a positive way? The responder believes, "The sermon could be beneficial to any church community. All believers should know that they are not alone. Also, believers should that other believers go through and face trials of the same. The sermon clearly allows a believer to see that what God does for one, He will do for another. No trial will be greater than the strength of the believer

First Responder, Question Four: Could the sermons easily become an inspirational tool for reaching none church goers? The responders says, "The Sermon was plain enough and taught in a way that all hears could take as a foundation to stand on in reaching non church goers."

First Responder, Question Five: Was the sermon overall beneficial to all age groups for your church setting? Advocates that, "Yes, Any church setting should have gotten spiritual understanding from the sermon.

First Responder, Question Six: What challenges were presented to the church that would transform your church into better witnesses for Christ? Views shows, "The challenge of going through trials and tribulations and know where to put your trust doing those times."

First Responder, Question Seven: Was there enough emphasis given in the message for improving the leadership roles in your church? Lastly, the responder highlight of the sermon emphatically affirms, "Yes, The message emphasized the importance of improving leadership roles by seeking and following God's guidance in every single task put before us."

Second Responder:

Sunday January 10, 2016

Text: First Corinthians 10:9-13

Subject: God Want Put No More on You Then You Can Bear

I.   Planning for Temptation

II.   God's Purpose for Your Test

III.   God's Will Help You Prevail in Your Temptation

Sunday: January 17, 2016

Text: Second Corinthians 12:7-9

Subject: When Stuff Isn't Going Your Way, You Can Count On God

I.   When Stuff Isn't Going Your Way, During Life's Tests

II.   When Stuff Isn't Going Your Way, You Can Count on God Grace

III.   When Stuff Isn't Going Your Way, You Can Have Victory in God.

Second Responder: Did the sermon regarding the importance pastoring and leadership impact the church? In response, "The church will have to go through some storms. However, God is with His church during the bad times. God will lead us through."

Second Responder, Question Two: Did the sermon based on the Apostle Paul's message to the early church address the spiritual needs of today's church? She argues, "Yes, Paul's writing to the church because he understood the church problems just as today's churches have problem."

Second Responder, Question Three: In your observations, how could the sermon benefit church communities in a positive way? Stating in effect, Learning how to deal with trials as you're going through and a believer can count it all joy when going through tests."

Second Responder, Question Four: Could the sermons easily become an inspirational tool for reaching none church goers? Agreeably, "Yes, Pastor Elzie made it simple and plain. He used the example of a diamond when miners find them as rough stones, and the diamond master take it a finishes taking it through the process of hammering and polishing it becomes a stone of much value."

Second Responder, Question Five: Was the sermon overall beneficial to all age groups for your church setting? The responder states, "Yes, Pastor Elzie made the sermon simple enough for believers of all age groups, including the younger generation to grasp the meaning if having to go through tough times."

Second Responder, Question Six: What challenges were presented to the church that would transform your church into better witnesses for Christ? The responder believes, "That there would always be suffering, test and trials, but if we remain faithful God will supply whatever we need."

Second Responder, Question Seven: Was there enough emphasis given in the message for improving the leadership roles in your church? The responder argues in the affirmative, "Yes, Pastor Elzie stated leader should not focus too much on the problem, but instead staying focused of God. Pastor Elzie the leaders of the church to learn too lean and depend on the Lord. Believing that, no problem is too big for Him to handle. He also stated that if the church is going to get better, that, "Love is the glue" that holds the church together."

Third Responder:

Sunday January 10, 2016

Text: First Corinthians 10:9-13

Subject: God Want Put No More on You Then You Can Bear

    I.   Planning for Temptation

    II.   God's Purpose for Your Test

    III.   God's Will Help You Prevail in Your Temptation

Sunday: January 17, 2016

Text: Second Corinthians 12:7-9

Subject: When Stuff Isn't Going Your Way, You Can Count On God

    I.   When Stuff Isn't Going Your Way, During Life's Tests

    II.   When Stuff Isn't Going Your Way, You Can Count on God Grace

    III. When Stuff Isn't Going Your Way, You Can Have Victory in God.

Third Responder, Question One: Did the sermon regarding the importance pastoring and leadership impact the church? The responder argues, "I believe that a Christian Church leader is responsible to lead God's flock by walking personally with God and

119

working together to help his sheep do the same. Our Bible sums it up with two great commandments, which are related: This simple means that leaders of God must work hard at helping their members relate to one another in love too! So, in response to the question, yes your leadership impacts the church because we can see the new member growth, bible study growth, Sunday school and worship service growth."

Third Responder, Question two: Did the sermon based on the Apostle Paul's message to the early church address the spiritual needs of today's church? This responder emphatically declares, "Yes! I believe that the Apostle Paul's message to the early church addressed the spiritual needs of today's church because we as a people, are living in dangerous and struggling times. Paul wanted us to know that he was dealing with a lot of stuff, but he said that God's Grace was available and that it was all we needed.

Just like the Sunday school Lesson, "Broken Relationship," here we see that God teaches us a lesson through the nation of Judah and Israel. He used a husband and wife to speak of His love for His people. Just as we must do in today's church. We must learn to love and forgive. We cannot go around holding grudges against people because that's not Christlike. We should ask ourselves what would Jesus do? Would you want God to never forgive?"

Third Responder, Question Three: In your observations, how could the sermon benefit church communities in a positive way? This responding participant observed that, "I believe that whether one goes to church or not, there will be talk no matter what.

Regardless of how one views a church, people expect their problems can be addressed in some way through the church. People expect the church to provide Bible-based answers that no one else can provide.

A church is the lifeline of any society and it is a unique place that should instill change in the community and the lives of people. The church is where people need to have their spiritual, physical and emotional needs met.

Example: Sometimes people come to church with broken spirit and a lot on their minds. If the leader of the church can't give encouraging words or uplift them, then they still are not receiving anything."

Third Responder, Question Four: Could the sermons easily become an inspirational tool for reaching none church goers? The responder states, "In my opinion, sermons can become an inspirational tool for reaching non church goers. I do believe that sermons can be a helpful teaching tool when used appropriately and in moderation. However, today's modern church is design to reach and help believers and it should focus on helping non believers. One can teach and preach all day long, but if you haven't taught your church about ministering to people who don't go to church, that like preaching you want to lose weight but constantly eating Big Macs!"

Third Responder, Question Five: Was the sermon overall beneficial to all age groups for your church setting? The responder stresses, "Yes, the sermon was definitely beneficial to all of the church. It was easy enough for my 10 year old to understand that if she's having a problem in her studies at school, all she has to do is pray and depend on God to answer all her needs. Even the middle (teenage), adults, and the elderly could gather that in times of trouble you need to cast all your cares on Him for He cares for you! We need to do just as Paul, never stop praying to God. We need to know that His grace is sufficient!"

Third Responder, Question Six: What challenges were presented to the church that would transform your church into better witnesses for Christ? The responder agreeable argues, "As a church, we were challenged to fall on our knees and pray instead of keeping thing bottled up inside. Whatever we're going through something we need to know how to do just as Paul did, never stop praying! We shouldn't put on pitty patty parties, but instead a praise party. When we can see that prayers are being answered, we can go out into the world and witness to others of the goodness of the Lord."

Third Responder, Question Seven: Was there enough emphasis given in the message for improving the leadership roles in your church? In response of the survey, the responder concludes by saying, "Our pastor set a good example for leadership roles in the church. He lead by example because he there for Bible Study, Sunday School, he visits the sick and shut-in and he's always on time! He always stresses the importance of being the best leader you can be if you hold a leadership role in the church. You can't lead if you are falling short. You must lead by example!"

Fourth Responder:

Sunday January 10, 2016

Text: First Corinthians 10:9-13

Subject: God Want Put No More on You Then You Can Bear

I.   Planning for Temptation

II.   God's Purpose for Your Test

III.   God's Will Help You Prevail in Your Temptation

Sunday: January 17, 2016

Text: Second Corinthians 12:7-9

Subject: When Stuff Isn't Going Your Way, You Can Count On God

I.   When Stuff Isn't Going Your Way, During Life's Tests

II.   When Stuff Isn't Going Your Way, You Can Count on God Grace

III.   When Stuff Isn't Going Your Way, You Can Have Victory in God.

Fourth Responder, Question One: Did the sermon regarding the importance pastoring and leadership impact the church? In response says, "I feel that the sermon had a great impact on the congregation. The Pastor emphasized the fact that God would not put more on them than they would be able to bear. This would serve as an admonition to recognize the situations or areas that causes trouble and that God would not let them be tempted beyond what they were able, and He would provide a way of escape. This also gave the congregation confidence to face any problem that they may encounter."

Fourth Responder, Question two: Did the sermon based on the Apostle Paul's message to the early church address the spiritual needs of today's church? Say, "Yes, The text taken from First Corinthians 10:9-13 and Second Corinthians 12:7-9. The sermon focused on the spiritual needs of today's Church and her effectiveness on the local church community. Each sermon emphasized the importance of keeping one faith in Jesus Christ even in the midst of trials and tribulations. The Church need to know that there is always someone that they can depend on when problems in their lives seem to be spiraling out of control. That Person is Jesus Christ."

Fourth Responder, Question Three: In your observations, how could the sermon benefit church communities in a positive way? The responder asserts, "In the sermon the pastor talked about Paul's struggle with his infirmities. He reminded the congregation of God's ever present grace. The church today may be affected by thorns in one form or another, but we can wait on the Lord with the knowledge that His grace is sufficient for us."

Fourth Responder, Question Four: Could the sermons easily become an inspirational tool for reaching none church goers? The responder argues," Non-church goers can take from the sermon's message that Paul was covered by God's grace irregardless to the to the thorns in the flesh. In knowing that God's grace was sufficient for Paul and hearing about the life, death, burial and resurrection of Christ, non-church goers may feel that they can turn their lives over to Christ."

Fourth Responder, Question Five: Was the sermon overall beneficial to all age groups for your church setting? The responder observed, "The sermon was beneficial to all ages, even the young children are impacted with struggles especially peer pressure. The pastor's sermon encouraged them to stand firm on their beliefs and don't give in to the pressures that they face."

Fourth Responder, Question Six: What challenges were presented to the church that would transform your church into better witnesses for Christ? The surveyors states, "The congregation was challenged with the need to bring love back into God's Church. The pastor gave instructions on how love will hold the church together in times of struggles. A church that has love will serve as light to enlighten the world of God's strength and power.

Fourth Responder, Question Seven: Was there enough emphasis given in the message for improving the leadership roles in your church? The responder says, "I strongly believe that the contents of the message served to encourage the leaders of the church to re-evaluate their roles and strive to improve them."

Addendum Analysis of the Survey

As observed by each of the responders' analysis and honest input regarding the state of the church community, they have concluded that with the best of effort from a biblical perspective there remains much work which needs to be done in the ecclesiologic realm of twenty-first century church community. For example, question number one of the questionnaires, all four responders agree there is room for improvement in all areas of church leadership.

In question two, the text surveys view biblical styles of preaching for pastoral leadership in the pulpit lifts the spiritual, physical, and emotional well-being of every Christian of the church congregation. As a positive response also, the pastoral leadership approach of dealing with the church and each worshipper's problem, they believe that the biblical presentation of Jesus as the Son of God who came as the incarnated Christ and invaded His own created world, was crucified on a Roman cross, buried in the tomb for three days, rose from the dead Sunday morning, and according to the Book of Acts Chapter One ascended into heaven on a cloud.

Question three, all four of the responders affirms, that, the church community were impacted in a positive way through the biblical style of preaching and which is how pastors should implement their spiritual skills of pastoral leadership which God has gifted them with as His called servants.

The responders for question four did not respond in detail the depth the extent of their conversation, however each believe that the sermons listed in this survey were simple enough that the congregation's small children were able to some extent relate to the pastor and the biblical message.

The fifth question comments from the four responders were limited but important to the ongoing process of building style for preaching in pastoral leadership.

With the sixth question, all agreed trusting God in the tests and trials of life is God's way of making better and faithful believers of Jesus Christ.

Finally, the matter of leadership from the responder's viewpoint believes that, leaders of the church should make improving the leadership roles a priority for the continuous growth and spiritual well-being of a local church.

In light of the responders survey in the previous appendix if the church is to remain spiritually active and necessary in the twenty-first century to address the world's frustrating and perplexing problems there must be a spirit urgency driven by pastoral leaders willing to take on the role of managing church through biblical styles of preaching which accompanies the pastoral leadership roles in the church community.

The Pastor Dilemma

Chapter Ten: Managing the Church

We previously discussed the divine calling of the pastor, and who they are from both the biblical definition and their role identity given by theological writers. Now the focus of the pastoral role of church manager is the primary objective of this chapter.

One major flaw of the twenty-first century church is the lack of leadership management. In the first century church in her infancy had few problems with administration and management. The Book of Acts Chapter 2:42-47 reveals the church acted as a family communal that were based on unwritten guidelines. She acted and responded upon the leadership of her first church pastors and especially the empowering influence of the Holy Spirit.

Pastors relied upon the leadership of God's Spirit to lead them in their role as administrators of God's church. In light of first century church leaders, they viewed the art of communication as a major factor for biblically leading the church even though by modern day standers their type of church leading is foreign to the twenty-first century forums. On the other hand, those leaders of the early church accomplished missions in short periods compared to the modern day church. Again, what needs to be recognized is the mode of the communication factor.

Communication is everything! In fact, Robert P. Cort, *Communicating With Employees* argues, "Communicating can be defined as the chain of understanding which permeates an organization from top to bottom, from bottom to top, and from side to side, and which moves the organization ahead toward its stated objectives. It is the cohesive force which holds the group together..."[110] In addition, biblical accounts reveals communication was imperative for effective pastoral leadership. For example, there were encamped in the Wilderness of Sinai approximately two-millions plus who had problems needing Moses attention. In Exodus 18:13-26 Jethro, the father-in-law of Moses observed that Moses' task of managing and administrating over grievances had become over challenging for the man of God to handle. However,

The pastor if they are to maintain a biblical styles of pastoral leadership it would be wise of them to note the leadership given by Moses' father-in-law who advise Israel's leader, number one, "And Moses' father in law said unto him, The thing that thou doest is not good...(Ex 18:17, KJV)[111]. Second, "Thou wilt surely wear away, both thou, and this people that is with thee: for this thing is too heavy for thee; thou art not able to perform it thyself alone. Hearken now unto my voice, I will give thee counsel, and God shall be with thee:

---

[110] Cort, Robert P. *Communicating With Employees*. 8th ed. Waterford, Connecticut: Prince-Hall, Inc., MCMLXIII. p.1
[111] Exodus 18: 18-19 King James Version

Be thou for the people to Godward, that thou mayest bring the causes unto God…" (Ex 18:18-19, KJV).[112]

Finally, Jetro offered an alternative solution for Moses communication problem. He advised, "Moreover thou shalt provide out of all the people able men, such as fear God, men of truth, hating covetousness; and place such over them, to be rulers of thousands, and rulers of hundreds, rulers of fifties, and rulers of tens: And let them judge the people at all seasons: and it shall be, that every great matter they shall bring unto thee, but every small matter they shall judge: so shall it be easier for thyself, and they shall bear the burden with thee. If thou shalt do this thing, and God command thee so, then thou shalt be able to endure, and all this people shall also go to their place in peace" (Ex 18:21-23, KJV).[113]

Similarly the Apostles encountered management issues similar to those during the Old Testament Period, but through biblical principles the New Testament leader guided by the Holy Spirit were lead to delegate responsibilities to Holy Spirit filled, wisdom endue, men of good report from within the early church community men who could help the Apostles shoulder the temporal responsibilities of providing for the needs of the people. In this way the Apostles could focus on the effective mission of preaching the Gospel of Jesus Christ according to (Acts 6:1-7).

In the church community, today churches and leader are faced with comparable challenges that places enormous burden on

---

[112] Ezekiel 18:18-19 King James Version
[113] Ibid

the one person. It is no wonder that many pastoral leaders leave the ministry, or run the risk of suffering physical and psychological challenges during the course of their pastoral roles. In other words, the work of leading the church from a pastoral prospective can be more effective and healthier for its pastor and church members when there is communication and delegation of leadership is equally distributed among capable, but saved Christians of the Church.

As to the dimensions of developing a particular style of preaching as pastoral-leader, individual pastors have the challenge of creating a mission focused style of preaching and pastoring that is uniquely their own. Dr. Larry L. McCall, *Effective Church Management: Discovering and Implementing Biblical Approach to Church Management* the class instructor for the National Baptist Congress of Christian Workers of the National Baptist Convention of America, Incorporated, during its June session in Tampa, Florida in the year 1999, argued, "The pastor must always keep the kingly, or management, role in prospective in relation to the prophetic and priestly role. He or she must also be careful not to place too much high value the church as an institution... Management is simply a component within the organization charged with the responsibility of enabling all the resources and functions of the organization to be utilized in establishing it mission and facilitating movement toward it."

Adding to that, each pastor must work as a biblical leader and learn their craft well enough to maneuver within their God-given personalities and spiritual gifts afforded them in their call servants of God. Applicable to the organizational structure, the pastor's prospective of God's church they must maintain a more loftier and holistic views of that which God has build, that being a holy organism with meaning and life housing born again believers as members in the church community.

One of the taxing problems of pastoring is losing sight of the importance of each church member as viable and needful church resources. In their daily contact with people in general pastors will need to develop a persona as a "people person" in other words, consciously learning how to become an expert at becoming "a good mixer." Paul the Apostle, said, "Do not neglect to show hospitality to strangers, for thereby some have entertained angels unawares" (Heb 13:2, RSV).[114]

Similarly, a pastor's ability to communicate revolves around the enter acting of the Holy Spirit. In saying that, there is a certain spiritual beauty that adorns the pastoral minister's personality. In the presence of other Christians, and no-believers his projection of Christ the spirit if the Lord toward those they come into contact with. This is the picture that reveals the early disciple in the writings of the Book of Acts as the writer Luke said, " When the Council saw the boldness of Peter and John and could see that they were obviously uneducated non-professionals, they were amazed and realized what being with Jesus had done for them" (Acts 4:13-14, TLB)! [115]

---

[114] Hebrews 13:2 Revised Standard Version
[115] Acts 4: 13-14 The Living Bible

Therefore the Christian pastoral leaders shoulder a great responsibility of emulating Jesus Christ. After all, He is the only pattern sufficient for Christian leaders to build a biblical style for preaching for pastoral leadership in this age of man's ultimate objectives for becoming more like the image of Christ and moving toward the end of the spiritual man's quest of maturing in Christ Jesus. In fact, without these two objective managing and leading a church become more of a chore than a joy of serving the Lord.

Herein, as Christians whom God has called to be pastoral His voiceS that make His Word come alive in biblical preaching through the pastoral ministry, we must realize and come to terms that we are citizens of two world. We are as the framers of a lost world, are the sojourner citizens in the temporal world and an eternal world. And as such, it is our God ordained calling to move about them and live as Christian leaders pointing the lost to Jesus Christ by declaring to them the birth, death, resurrection and His ascension into heaven.

Bibliography

Arnold, Bill T., and Bryant E. Beyer. *Encountering the Old Testament*. Grand Rapids, Michigan: Baker Books, 1999. Print.

Bancroft, Emery H. *CHRISTIAN THEOLOGY: Systematic and Biblical*. 2nd Revised Ed. 1976 ed. Grand Rapids, Michigan: Zondervan Publishing House, 1929.

Barnette, Henlee H. *Introducing Christian Ethics*. Nashville, Tennessee: Broadman Press, 1961. Print.

Baxter, J. Sidlow. *Explore the Book*. Grand Rapids, Michigan: Zondervan Publishing House, 1960.

Bickers, Dennis. *The Healthy Pastor: Easing the Pressures of Ministry*. Kansas City: Beacon Hill Press, 2010. Print.

Bowman, Samuel L. *Preaching in the Capital*. Nashville, Tennessee: Sunday School Publishing Board National Baptist Convention, U. S. A., Inc., 1993. unk.

Bullinger, E. W. *A Critical Lexicon and Concordance to the English and Greek New Testament*. Grand Rapids, Michigan: Kregel Publications, 1999. Print.

Cairns, Earle E. *Christianity Through The Centuries: A History of the Christian Church*. 1982 28th Rev. ed. Grand Rapids, Michigan: Academic Books-Zondervan Publishing House, 1982.

Christian Post. N.p, December 17, 2013. Web. 2015 December 06. www.christianpost.com/news/pastors-mental-illness-and-suicide.

Cort, Robert P. *Communicating With Employees*. 8th ed. Waterford, Connecticut: Prince-Hall, Inc., MCMLXIII. Not in Print.

Criswell, W. A. *The Chriswell Study Bible*. 3rd ed. Nashville, Camden, New York: Thomas Nelson, Publishers, 1979. Print.

Dawn, Marva J., and Eugene H. Peterson. *The Unnecessary Pastor: Rediscovering the Call*. Grand Rapids, Michigan/ Cambridge U. K.: William B. Eerdmans Publishing Company, 2000. Print.

Elwell, Walter A., and Robert W. Yarbrough. *Encountering the New Testament: A Historical and Theological Survey*. Second ed. Grand Rapids, Michigan: BakerAcademic, 1998, 2005. Print.

Gilbertson, Jim. *Biblesoft Version 5*. ed. Seattle, Washington: Biblesoft, 1988-2006. 5.

Hester, H. I. *THE HEART OF THE NEW TESTAMENT*. Thirty-Fourth ed. 1980 ed. Nashville, Tennessee: Broadman Press, 1980. Print.

Hicks, Jr., H. Beecher. *Correspondence with a Cripple From Tarsus*. Grand Rapids, Michigan: Zondervan Publishing House, 1990. Print.

Hicks, Jr., H. Beecher. *Preaching Through A Storm*. Grand Rapids, Michigan: Zondervan, 1987. Print.

Hitchens, Christopher. *god is not Great: How Religion Poisons Everything*. New York, NY: Twelve Hachette Book Group, 2007. Print.

Largent, Brent. *(Seminar) Survey of First and Second Thessalonians*. Theological Studies, Newburgh Theological Seminary and College of the Bible, 2009. Web. 11 April, 2011. <http://www.newburghseminary.com>.

LaRue, Cleophus J. *I Believe I'll Testify: The Art of African American Preaching*. 1st ed. Louisville, Kentucky: Westminister John Knox Press, 2011. Print.

Lockyer, Herbert. *ALL THE APOSTLES OF THE BIBLE*. Grand Rapids, Michigan: Zondervan Publishing House, 1972. Print.

Maxwell, John. *There's No Such Thing as Business Ethics: There is Only One Rule for Making Decisions*. : Center Street a division of Hachette Group, 2003. Print.

McIntosh, Gary, and Glen Martin. *Finding Them, Keeping: Effective Strategies for Evangelism and Assimilation in the Local Church*. Nashville: Broadman & Holman Publishers, 1992. Print.

Mellette, Glenn W. *Church Growth 101: A Church Growth Guidebook for Ministers and Laity*. Newburgh, Indiana: Newburgh Press, 2012. Print.

Oden, Thomas C. *Pastoral Theology: Essentials of Ministry*. New York, NY: HaperCollins Publishers, 1983. Print.

Pattison, T. Harwood. *The Making of the Sermon: For the Class-Room and the Study*. Philadelphia: American Baptist Publication Society, 1902. Print.

Peterson, Eugene H. *THE MESSAGE: The Bible in Contemporary Language*. Seattle, Washington: : Biblesoft , 2002. PC Study Bible V.5.

Pfeiffer, Charles F., Howard F. Vos, and John Rea, eds. *Wycliffe Bible Encyclopedia*. Fourth Printing, 1979 ed. Chicago: Moody Press, 1975. Print.

Polhill, John B. *Paul and His Letters*. Nashville, Tennessee: B&H Publishing Group, 1999. Print.

Scroggie, W. Graham. *THE UNFOLD DRAMA OF REDEMPTION*. Grand Rapids, Michigan USA: Kregel Publications, 1994. Print.

Smith, Roy L. *Know Your Bible Series Study Number Eight*. New York - Nashville: Abingdon-Cokesbury Press, 1944. Print.

Stedman, Ray C., and Denney D. James. *God's Loving Word: Exploring the Gospel of John*. Grand Rapids, Michigan: Discovery House Publishers, 1993. Print.

Tenny, Merrill C. *New Testament Survey Revised*. 2nd Rev. 1961 ed. Grand Rapids, Michigan: WM. B.EERDMANS PUBLISHING COMPANY, 1961. Print.

Thompson, James W. *Pastoral Ministry according to Paul: A Biblical Vision*. Grand Rapids, Michigan: Bakers Academic, 2006. Print.

Nollen Elzie Sr. PhD

Vines, Jerry, and Jim Shaddix. *Power in the Pulpit: How to Prepare and Deliver Expository Sermons*. Chicago: MOODY PUBLISHERS, 1999. Print.

Willmington, Harold. *Willmington's Bible Handbook*. : P C Biblesoft, 1988-2006. C D 5.

---. *Willmington's Bible Handbook*. Wheaton, Illinois: Tyndale House Publishers, Inc, 1997. PC Biblesoft V.5.

The Pastor Dilemma